ELEMENTA

TEACHING LITERACY WITH LATIN

ACKNOWLEDGMENTS:

Curriculum Designer .... Jamel Daugherty

Editors .... Elizabeth W. Butterworth, Marco Romani Mistretta

Contributors .... Kaitlyn Boulding, Coleman Connelly, Allegra Forbes,
Kimberly Paton, Alexander Petkas

Literacy Consultant .... CQ Wilder, M.Ed

Graphic Designer .... Megan Prom

Elementa: Teaching Literacy with Latin is an introductory Latin course designed to reinforce English literacy skills. The curriculum is a publication of the Paideia Institute, a non-profit educational organization that promotes the study of the classical humanities through programming in the US and abroad.

This curriculum is part of The Paideia Institute's Aequora initiative, founded in Brooklyn, NY in 2013 to promote the study of Latin at the elementary level. The Paideia Institute collaborates with high school and university classics departments to run Latin enrichment classes in public schools, libraries, and community centers nationwide.

The production of this curriculum was funded in part by the Onassis Foundation USA, the Achelis & Bodman Foundation, and the Beginning with Children Charter School in Brooklyn, NY.

Special thanks are due to the participants in The Paideia Institute's Summer Humanities Internship program, who contributed content to the curriculum during the 2016, 2017, 2018, 2019, and 2020 editions of the program.

Tel. 609.429.0734

http://www.paideiainstitute.org/

THE PAIDEIA INSTITUTE
75 VARICK STREET, 11TH FLOOR
NEW YORK, NY 10013

ISBN 978-1-7324750-8-3

TABLE OF CONTENTS:

INTRODUCTION

Welcome to the Paideia Institute's *Elementa* curriculum. *Elementa* is designed to be an engaging, relevant, and inclusive introductory Latin curriculum. Through *Elementa*, we strive to expand access to the Latin language and the cultures and mythology of the ancient Mediterranean world. The curriculum is shaped by our belief that everyone should have access to Latin and the classical tradition and, importantly, to joyful and connected learning experiences. To that end, a key element of the curriculum is fun. Within this textbook you will find interactive exercises, creative activities, skits, and mythological and historical narratives that encourage you to claim and define the Latin language and the ancient world as your own.

The *Elementa* textbook includes eleven units and three additional lessons on "Elements of Literacy." Each unit is composed of three main sections: a grammar lesson focusing on a Latin part of speech (accompanied by a vocabulary chart), a culture lesson centered on a key element of ancient Roman history or society, and a mythology lesson based on a narrative that allows you to place the vocabulary you learn into an appropriate context.

The *Elementa* curriculum was born in 2018 as the successor of Aequora, the Paideia Institute's after-school classical enrichment program. Aequora began as a volunteer-based program to promote the study of Latin at the elementary and middle school level. The program has now expanded into a nationwide outreach initiative that continues to foster fruitful collaborations between colleges or high schools offering Latin and local K-8 schools or community centers interested in incorporating Latin into their after-school education.

Why Latin? About 65% of English vocabulary is based on Latin, and the figure rises to 90% if one considers the impact of Classical languages on multisyllabic words alone (see T. Green, *e Greek and Latin Roots of English*, London 2015). As a result, a single Latin root or morpheme can aid in the understanding and acquisition of twenty or more English words. Recent pedagogical research shows that first-year Latin instruction improves students' ability to read English by +150% compared to students without Latin, and that 80% of students with Latin score better on standardized tests than the control group of their peers without Latin (data from the FLES Latin program evaluation reports). Furthermore, over 80% of Spanish vocabulary derives directly from Latin, and the *Elementa* curriculum helps native Spanish speakers understand the logic of their language and its connections to English. Statistical studies show that teaching English learners Latin roots helps them to discover the meaning of English words they do not know through problem solving (A. Crosson et al., *Extending the Bounds of Morphology Instruction*, "Reading & Writing" 2018).

Besides its power to enrich literacy and improve outcomes on standardized tests, Latin also provides a key to access a virtually inexhaustible wealth of knowledge and discovery made possible by the ancient world and its legacy in the modern age. Classical antiquity, in fact, has stimulated people's curiosity for centuries and continues to do so in our times. Through *Elementa*, we teach the basics of Latin grammar and vocabulary in such a way that Latin provides students with the tools to improve their mastery of English and Spanish (and other languages!), but an equally crucial goal of the curriculum is to expose students to Roman culture and inspire curiosity for the ancient world at large.

Upon completion of the curriculum, students will be able to:

- Recall basic Latin phrases and a vocabulary of 150+ Latin words.

- Identify the parts of speech in a Latin or English sentence.

- Critically discuss aspects of Roman culture and its influence on the present.

- Recognize major characters and narratives from classical mythology and analyze its influence on contemporary literature and popular culture.

- Correctly determine the meanings of English and Spanish words and build vocabulary by using knowledge of Latin roots and affixes.

Vocabulary

LATINE	ESPAÑOL	ENGLISH
Salve	Saludos (a una persona)	Hello (to one person)
Salvete	Saludos (a muchas personas)	Hello (to more than one person)
Quid tibi nomen est?	¿Cuál es tu nombre?	What is your name?
Mihi nomen est . . .	Mi nombre es . . .	My name is
Gratias	Gracias	Thank you
Nihil est	De nada	It's nothing (You're welcome)
Quid agis?	¿Cómo estás?	How are you?
Ago bene	Estoy bien	I'm well
Ago male	Estoy mal	I'm bad
Ago optime	Estoy muy bien (optimo)	I feel great
Ago pessime	Estoy muy mal (pésimo)	I feel horrible
Vale, Valete	Adios	Farewell

CULTURAL CONNECTION

As you can see from the vocabulary in this section, there are words in Spanish that are very similar to the words in Latin.

Why is this so? In 146 BCE, the Greek Peninsula first came under Roman control, and around 200 BCE, the Romans colonized the Iberian Peninsula, also called Hispania (the name given by the Romans to modern-day Spain and Portugal). As the Romans conquered these territories, they also brought their language, Latin, to the inhabitants of the region. Over time, Latin evolved to incorporate Greek influences and later developed into the Spanish we speak today. Throughout this text, we have included Greek and Spanish alongside the Latin and English vocabulary so you can make your own comparisons. You will find even more connections to Greek, Spanish, and other languages in *Culture Connections*.

En 146 BCE, la península griega cayó bajo el control romano por la primera vez. Alrededor de 200 BCE, los romanos tomar‐ control de la península ibérica, o Hispania, y trajeron con ello‐ su idioma—el latín. Con tiempo, el latín empezó a incorporar influencia griega y, eventualmente, se convirtió en el español q‐ se habla hoy en día.

LESSON 1.1: Who were the Romans?

The Roman Empire had a powerful army which waged war with places like Egypt, North Africa, Greece, France, Spain, and Britain. People from all these places traveled to Rome, or met with Romans, and they shared customs, traditions, and ideas.

The map below shows all the places that were part of the Roman Empire.
Do you recognize any of the names of the places?

Can you guess what some of them are called today?

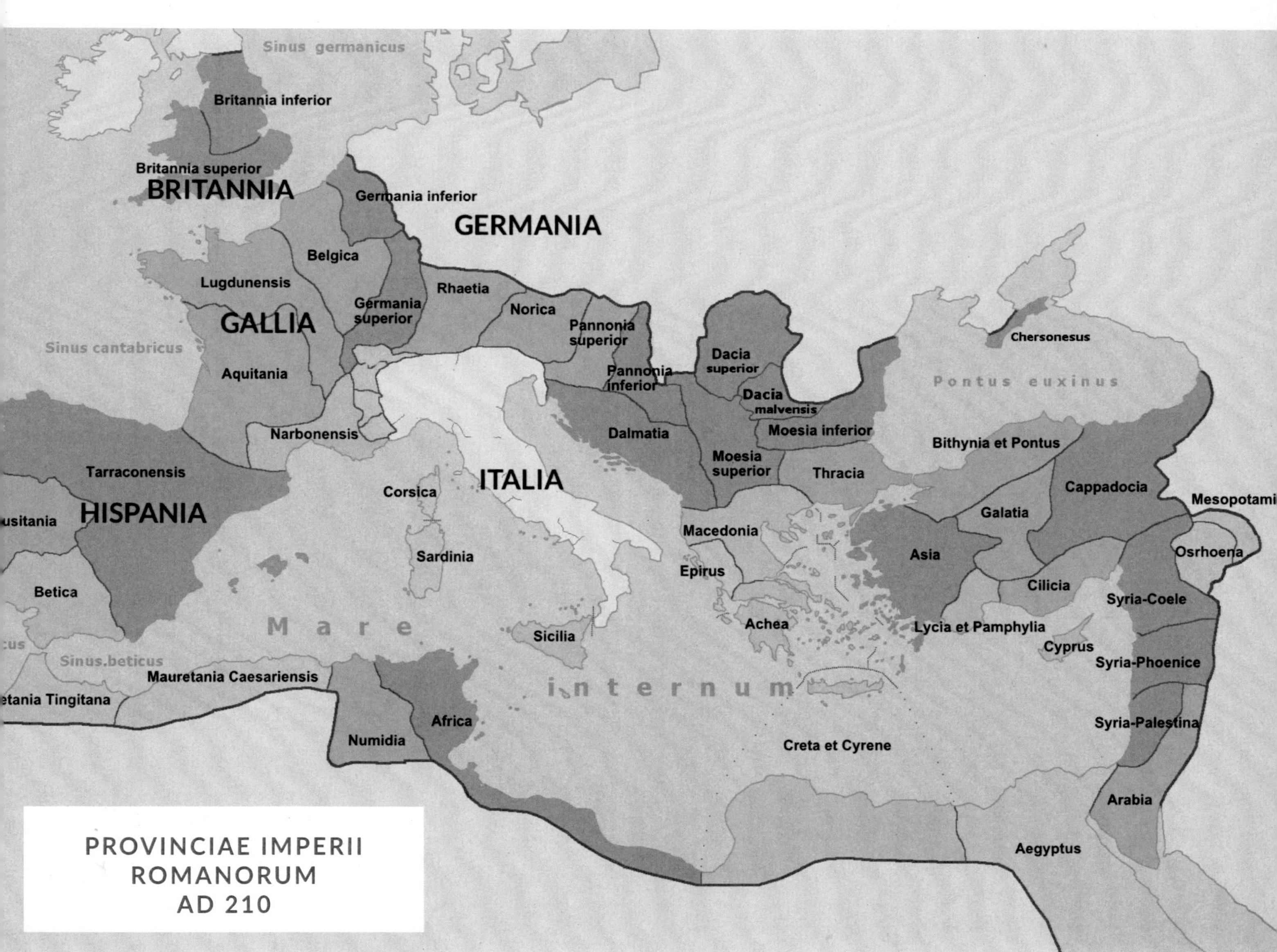

IT'S ALL GREEK TO ME! OR IS IT ROMAN?

The Greeks and Romans have many things in common—so many that it might be easy to get confused between the two—but these are actually two different civilizations. It's important to know who's who! Though they were neighbors, shared some mythological stories, and thrived roughly during the same span of history, they spoke different languages, had different systems of government, and had very different views of the world.

Can you think of two countries today that are geographically close and might share some cultural traits, but speak their own language and are distinct in their own ways?

GOVERNMENT

When we talk about the Greeks, we are referring to a collection of city-states that shared a similar culture and language. Each city-state operated with its own unique form of government and values. Often, the city-states would unite to defeat a common enemy, but sometimes they would fight amongst themselves too! Athens and Sparta frequently clashed as rival powers with contrasting cultures. Athens was ruled by a democracy, meaning every male citizen could vote on laws and decisions. Sparta was ruled by two kings and a council of elders, similar to Rome's republican form of government.

The Romans first developed as a monarchy—meaning they were ruled by kings. Later, they developed a republican form of government and ended with an empire ruled by emperors.

GEOGRAPHY

The Greeks were around long before the Romans expanded their empire, but eventually the Romans grew and conquered the Greeks. Check out the map to see how close they were as neighbors!

RELIGION

You may have noticed that the Greeks and Romans share mythological stories and have the "same" gods—just with different names. This is because they both believed in many gods—or polytheism. When they encountered a new god that was similar to one of their own, they assumed he was the same and absorbed all the stories and characteristics from the other god.

However, Romans and Greeks were very different in the ways that they worshipped and practiced their religion. The Romans were very formal, public, and ritualistic. The Greeks varied widely in how and who they worshipped, with many secret cults and mystical stories.

ART AND CULTURE

A famous Roman named Horace once wrote, "Graecia capta ferum victorem cepit," or "Captive Greece took captive her savage conqueror." He meant that although Rome conquered Greece, Greek culture and art thrived amongst the Romans who admired and adopted so much of the Greek culture. The Romans were known for being very practical and militaristic, while the Greeks loved beauty, creativity, and perfection in the arts.

LANGUAGE

The Romans spoke Latin. The Greeks spoke Greek. However, the Latin alphabet evolved from the same letters as the Greek alphabet! Many Romans learned Greek to be able to travel and do business with their neighbors, so other elements of the Greek language influenced Latin over time—just like English is influenced by Latin words.

Look at the timeline below and notice how we measure time between BCE (Before Common Era) and CE (Common Era). How many years ago from today was Rome founded?

TIMELINE OF ROMAN HISTORY

753 BCE 509 BCE 27 BCE 476 CE 1776 CE Today

REPUBLIC EMPIRE

MONARCHY

Some of the bolded terms below are Latin words that look similar to the English meaning—this is because those English words are derived from Latin! What do you think the terms mean?

Capitoline Wolf

In 509 BCE, the Romans overthrew their last king and became a **res publica** . In the time of the republic, the **populus** had the right to vote, but only if they were male Roman citizens.

In 27 BCE, the first **imperator**, Augustus, came to power, and that was the start of the Roman Empire. The Roman Empire had a powerful army which waged war with places like Egypt, North Africa, Greece, France, Spain, and Great Britain. People from all these places came to live in the city of Rome and shared customs, traditions, and ideas.

Septimius Severus Emperor from 193-211 CE, born in modern day Libya

In 476 CE, the Roman empire had too many problems. They were invaded by **Germanic** tribes and the western half of the empire fell apart. The eastern half, called the Byzantine Empire, continued for about another thousand years until 1453. The Byzantines still considered themselves to be Romans throughout this time.

From the founding to the fall of Rome, how many years did Roman civilization last?

How many years has our own country existed?

You may recognize many aspects of Roman culture that seem familiar today. They invented and improved many things that we still use in everyday life, like concrete, aqueducts and sewers, bound books, and, in a modified form, the Julian calendar. But there are also many things

Roman Aqueduct

that are very different. As you read, imagine life in the ancient world and think about what we can learn from both the similarities and differences between us and the Romans.

We will be learning Latin, the language that the Romans spoke, which contains thousands of words and parts of words that we still use everyday!

EXERCISE 1.1

You have traveled back in time to Ancient Rome! Before you can enter the city, two Roman guards stop you and demand that you answer their questions. Use your vocabulary list to give an appropriate response to each comment or question below.

1. Salve!

Responde Latine

2. Quid tibi nomen est?

Responde Latine

3. Quid agis?

Responde Latine

4. Where in the empire are you from?

Responde Anglice

5. What year is it?

Responde Anglice

6. Gratias tibi agimus!

Responde Latine

7. Vale!

Responde Latine

Χαῖρε!

Χαῖρε! (pronounced KAI-ray) This is how you say "Hello!" to someone in Ancient Greek. Look out for more Greek words and trivia as you learn more Latin.

LESSON 1.2: Romance Languages and Derivatives

Have you ever wondered why some words sound similar in different languages? For example, to say *Thank you* is *gracias* in Spanish, *grazie* in Italian, and *gratias* in Latin. This is because these languages are related in one big language family! It may begin as one "mother" language, and then when people speak a language for a long time, they start pronouncing things differently and using new words. When the accents and words of two groups become so different that the groups can't understand each other anymore, we say that those groups are speaking two different languages—and little baby languages are born!

This is is how Latin turned into different languages in different parts of the Roman Empire, like Spain, France, and Italy. We call the languages that come from Latin **Romance languages** because they came from the Romans.

English does not belong in the Romance language family, but it lives next door and likes to borrow and play with words from its neighbors to make new words of its own. You can think of words like building blocks that are borrowed from the neighbors and combined with a different set of building blocks to make new words. These new words are called **derivatives**. For example, from the Latin word for thanks (*gratias*), we get English words like *grateful*, meaning "thankful" and *gratitude*, meaning "thankfulness." Do you see how the words are similar?

CULTURAL CONNECTION

Latin was used in Europe for a long time and influenced a great number of European languages like English and Spanish. We call languages like this, "classical." Similarly, classical Chinese was used throughout East Asia, including China, Japan, Korea and Vietnam, for almost two millennia and had a major impact on modern Mandarin, Japanese and Korean.

We study Latin today because it can help us understand the Romance languages that come from it, as well as the individual words, or derivatives, that are borrowed from it. Knowing where a word comes from is incredibly useful when learning vocabulary because if you know a word's original meaning, you might be able to guess pretty accurately what that word means today.

LATIN ROOT	ENGLISH DERIVATIVES	SPANISH
bene	benefactor, beneficial, benign, benefit, benevolent, benediction	bien, bueno, bien hacer
male	malady, malicious, malevolent, malaria, malnutrition, malignant	mal, malo, maldad
optime	optimize, optimism, optimistic, optimal	optimista, óptima
pessime	pessimist, pessimism, pessimistic	pesimista, pesimismo
nomen	nomenclature, nominal, nominate, misnomer, nominee, denominator	nombre, nominar, denominación

EXERCISE 1.2

Match each English derivative with its Latin root by writing the Latin root and its meaning in the chart below. All the words are from Unit 1 vocabulary. Then, underline, circle, or highlight the letters that the roots have in common with their English derivative. The first one has been completed for you.

LATIN ROOT	ENGLISH DERIVATIVES
<u>val</u>e = Be Well	pre**val**ent
	malady
	annihilate
	misnomer
	grateful

*In the following sentences, the **bold** words are English derivatives. Using your knowledge of their Latin roots, what do you think these words mean?*

1. The Roman people were **grateful** because Emperor Augustus brought peace to the city.

    a) Enthusiastic   b) Confused   c) Rude   d) Thankful

2. During the Gallic Wars, Julius Caesar **annihilated** his enemies.

    a) Completely wiped out   b) Greatly honored   c) Bravely fought   d) Fearfully escaped

3. German chocolate cake is a **misnomer** because it was invented by an American.

    a) Lawn gnome   b) Incorrect name   c) Sugary treat   d) Success

4. Even though I went to the doctor, I still do not know the cause of my **malady.**

    a) Illness, feeling bad   b) Mutation   c) Expensive bill   d) Sudden growth

ZOOM IN

In Ancient Greece, the goddess of victory was called Nike. (The Roman version was Victoria). The sportswear brand, Nike, took their name directly from this goddess. The Greeks and Romans had a tradition of victory, in both athletic competition and wars, and the company Nike hoped to copy this. What other reasons might Nike have to name themselves after victory?

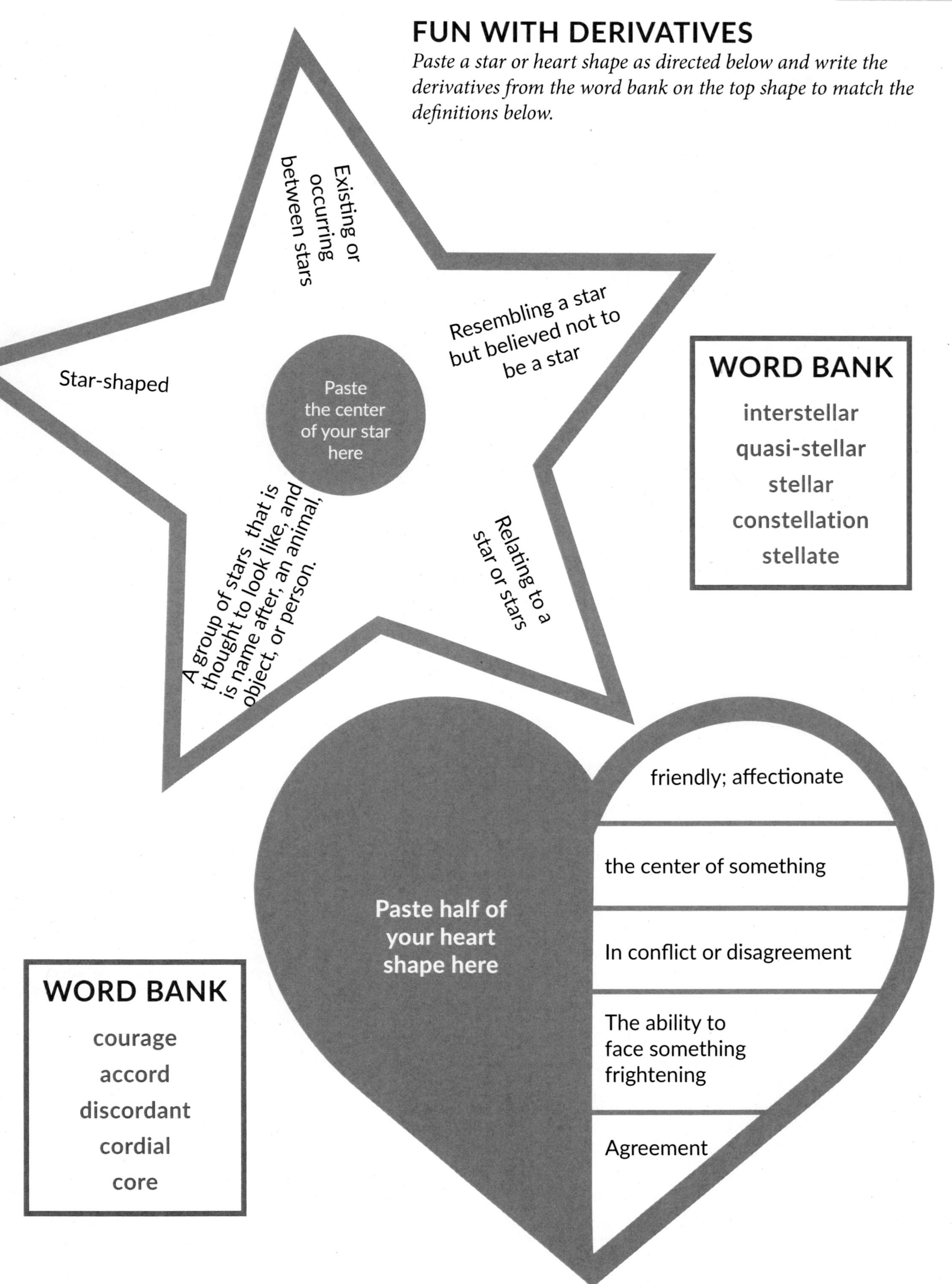
FUN WITH DERIVATIVES
Paste a star or heart shape as directed below and write the derivatives from the word bank on the top shape to match the definitions below.
Existing or occurring between stars
Resembling a star but believed not to be a star
Star-shaped
Paste the center of your star here
A group of stars that is thought to look like, and is name after, an animal, object, or person.
Relating to a star or stars
WORD BANK
interstellar
quasi-stellar
stellar
constellation
stellate
friendly; affectionate
the center of something
In conflict or disagreement
The ability to face something frightening
Agreement
Paste half of your heart shape here
WORD BANK
courage
accord
discordant
cordial
core

LESSON 1.3: What is Mythology?

The Latin word for myth is *fabula*. Our English word 'myth' comes from the Greek word *muthos*.

Myths are tales of gods, heroes, and monsters—and their interactions with people.

The myths that the Romans believed were very important to them. They helped the Romans understand what made them Roman and what was going on in the world around them. The woods, mountains, trees, and rivers where the Romans lived were seen as alive with divine forces. For example, Neptune (Poseidon) was the god of freshwaters and the sea so sailors would pray to him for safe voyages.

Roman fresco found at the Villa of Mysteries, Pompeii

Romans loved to make pictures of their gods and goddesses.

They painted frescoes of scenes from mythology and made beautiful statues out of marble.

CULTURAL CONNECTION

In Spanish, almost all of the days of the week come from the Latin names of the Roman gods. Also, the Spanish word for week, *semana*, comes from the Latin word for seven days, *septimana*!

ROMAN GOD	SPANISH	ENGLISH
Luna	Lunes	Monday
Mars	Martes	Tuesday
Mercury	Miércoles	Wednesday
Jupiter	Jueves	Thursday
Venus	Viernes	Friday
Saturn	Sábado	Saturday
Sol	Domingo	Sunday

EXERCISE 1.3

The Romans loved to portray their mythological stories in art. They decorated their walls with paintings called frescoes. Elaborate pictures were also made out of tiny tiles to create a mosaic that would decorate the floors.

Look at the Roman frescoes and mosaics and see if you can match each with the god or goddess that it is depicting.

______ 1. Jupiter, king of the gods

______ 2. Neptune, god of the sea

______ 3. Minerva, goddess of wisdom and military strategy

______ 4. Bacchus, god of wine and fertility

______ 5. Diana, goddess of the hunt

A 

B 

C 

D 

E 

Χαῖρε!

Have you noticed ways in which ancient myths influence our culture today? *Percy Jackson and the Olympians* by Rick Riordan is a series that follows the adventures of Percy and his friends. They discover that they are demigods, the children of gods and mortals. While navigating their lives, they encounter heroes, gods, and monsters.

ROMAN GODS FAMILY TREE

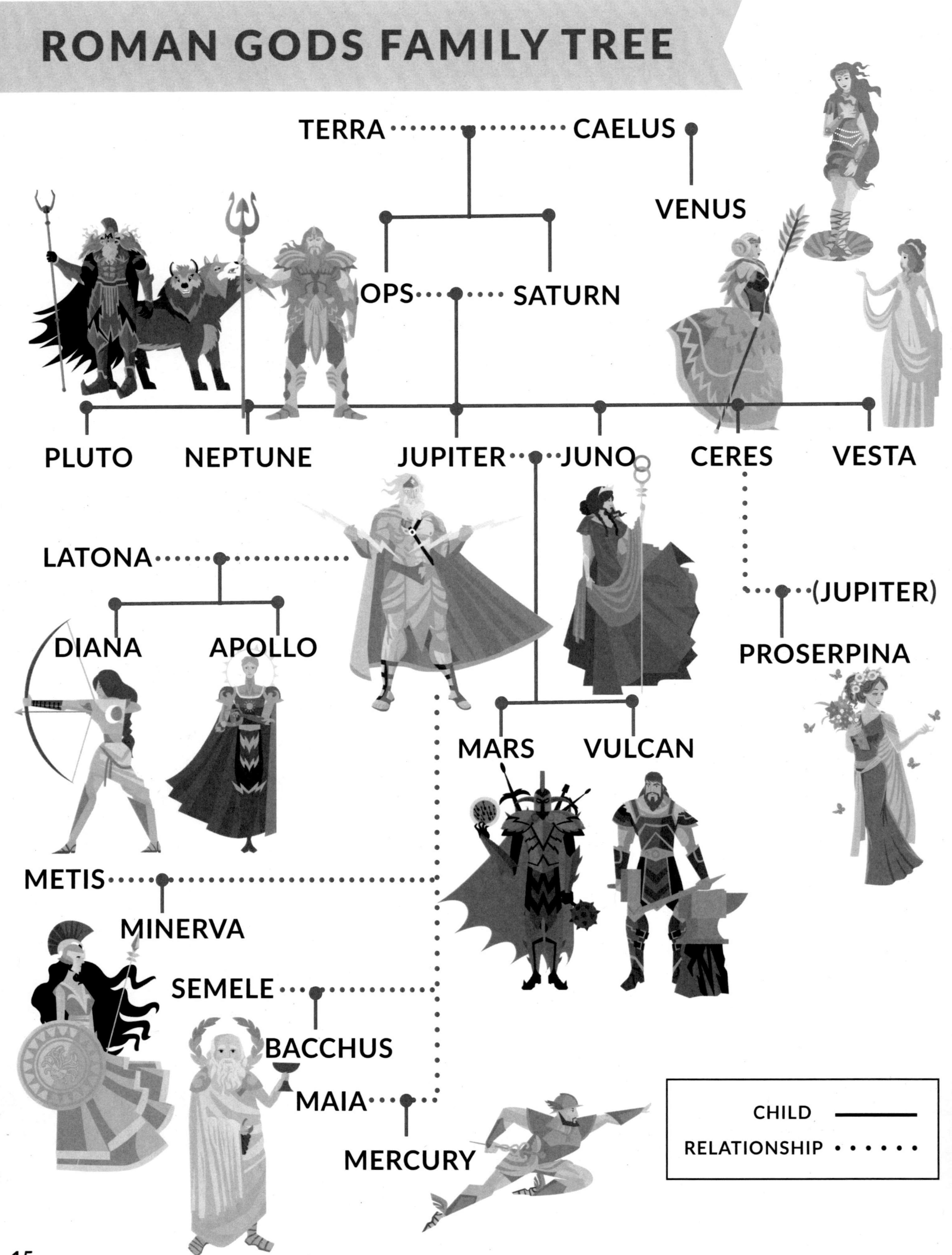

THE OLYMPIANS AND BEYOND

*The Greeks and Romans believed in **polytheism**, or many gods. When they encountered a god from another culture, they might identify it as one of their own, then absorb the stories and characteristics of that new god with the old. Over time, the Roman and Greek gods were thought to be the same and ruled over the same areas of nature, or domain. As you learn more about each god, use the bank below and hints throughout this book to fill in each domain.*

DOMAINS

the sea	sun, medicine, arts, music	love, beauty
wine, fertility, theater	marriage, childbirth	king of the gods, the sky
hearth, sacred fire	travel, mischief, messenger	the hunt, moon, wilderness
grain, harvest	blacksmiths, technology	war
the underworld	wisdom, arts, war strategy	

	ROMAN GOD	GREEK GOD	DOMAIN
1	Jupiter	Zeus	
2	Juno	Hera	
3	Neptune	Poseidon	
4	Pluto	Hades	
5	Mercury	Hermes	
6	Vulcan	Hephaestus	
7	Venus	Aphrodite	
8	Apollo	Apollo	
9	Minerva	Athena	
10	Diana	Artemis	
11	Mars	Ares	
12	Bacchus	Dionysius	
13	Vesta	Hestia	
14	Ceres	Demeter	

ADDITIONAL NOTES

Vocabulary

LATINE	ESPAÑOL	ENGLISH
avia	abuela	grandmother
avus	abuelo	grandfather
pater	padre	father
mater	madre	mother
filia	hija	daughter
puer	niño	boy
puella	niña	girl
frater	hermano	brother
soror	hermana	sister
domus	hogar, Casa	home
lupus	lobo	wolf
rex	rey	king
pastor	pastor	shepherd

Χαῖρε!

Did you know that the Ancient Greeks had their own alphabet? The first two letters are alpha (α) and beta (β). This is where our word alphabet comes from. Trace the letters below and try writing the alpha and beta on your own.

Αα   Ββ

LESSON 2.1: Nouns

PARTS OF SPEECH: WHAT IS A NOUN?

A **noun** is a _______________, _______________, _______________, or _____________ .

What are some examples for each of these in English?

______________ ______________ ______________ ______________

What are some examples in Spanish or other languages you know?

Sometimes Latin nouns will change their _________________ depending on how they are

used in a sentence, or if they are ____________________ or ____________________ .

Do English nouns do this? List some examples.

ZOOM IN

The trident, a common symbol in logos and modern culture, comes from weapon of the sea-god, Neptune. The car company Maserati has a trident as its logo. The founders say they were inspired by a statue of Neptune holding his trident. It also embodies strength and power, two characteristics that the car company wanted to have. What are some other reasons why the trident remains a common symbol?

EXERCISE 2.1

Oh no! The following derivatives have left their domus *and gotten lost. Help them find their way back to the correct Latin root by listing the derivatives that match together with their Latin root.*

domicile

matron

dome

matrimony

regimen

affiliate

filia

____

____

mater

regal

maternal

rex, regis

____

____

____

tyrannosaurus rex

filial

interregnum

domus

____

____

____

____

____

regent

domesticity

Imagine that you are part of a Roman **familia.** The Roman familia did not refer only to blood relatives, but to all members of a household. Adoption was common and other household members could include a **pater**, a **mater,** their **filius** (a son) or their **filia,** and sometimes other relatives and slaves.

The **pater** was the head of the **familia**, and he held great power called **patria potestas** (paternal power). The **mater** oversaw cooking and clothing production like spinning and weaving.

At seven years old, a **puer** might begin his education at school, and a **puella** would stay at home to learn how to sew, play music, and run the kitchen.

Most families in the city lived in buildings called **insulae**. Like many buildings in cities today, most insulae had shops on the bottom floor and apartments on the upper floors. An entire family might live in a one-room apartment.

SLAVERY IN ANCIENT ROME

Slavery was common in the ancient world, and slaves played an important role in Roman society. The Romans did not enslave one particular group of people; instead, the Romans would enslave various people of various ethnic groups after capturing them in war. Slaves worked in several industries, including mining, agriculture, housework, commerce, and construction. Greek slaves were especially valued for their intellectual abilities, and often taught Roman boys from wealthy families writing, rhetoric, and Greek to prepare them to become statesmen. Although slaves worked in many diverse areas of Roman life, all of the slaves were considered property, and were often treated harshly.

Sometimes owners freed their slaves and sometimes slaves were able to purchase their freedom. A freed slave had the right to vote in Rome, and the children of a freed slave were full Roman citizens and could be elected to public office.

Left, a row of insulae at Ostia, a port city near Rome.

Right, a row of modern apartments.

EXERCISE 2.2

Match each English derivative with its Latin root by writing the Latin root and its meaning in the chart below. All the words are from Unit 2 vocabulary. Then, underline, circle, or highlight the letters that the roots have in common with their English derivative. The first one has been completed for you.

LATIN ROOT	ENGLISH DERIVATIVES
soror = sister	sorority
	patriarch
	puerile
	interregnum
	lupine

In the following sentences the bolded words are English derivatives. Using your knowledge of their Latin roots, what do you think these words mean?

1. In college, some women might choose to join a **sorority**.

   a) gym   b) sisterhood   c) religious organization   d) academic competition

2. The **patriarch** of the family had to approve all major decisions.

   a) picky pet   b) financial advisor   c) grandmother   d) male leader

3. The teenagers were warned not to commit such **puerile** pranks again.

   a) immature, juvenile   b) dangerous, harmful   c) costly, expensive   d) brief

4. Oliver Cromwell was a leader in England during the **interregnum**.

   a) period between kings   b) famine   c) 17th century   d) revolutionary time

5. Cassius had a **lupine** grin that made Brutus wary of him.

   a) shark-like   b) evil   c) wolf-like   d) weaselly

LESSON 2.3: Romulus and Remus

Rome has been around for a very, very long time. But if you travel back in time a very, very, very, very long time you will only find fields and **pastores**.

A long time ago, there was a **rex** named Numitor who had a **filia** named Rhea Silvia in a kingdom called Alba Longa. Numitor's evil **frater**, Amulius, wanted to be **rex**. This evil **frater** seized power and forced the **filia** of Numitor, Rhea Silvia, to become a vestal virgin. A vestal virgin was a priestess of the goddess Vesta who could not get married.

Mars, the Roman god of war, loved the **filia** of the **rex**. He made Rhea Silvia his wife, even though she was a vestal virgin. Rhea soon gave birth to two **pueri**: Romulus and Remus. Romulus and Remus were twin **fratres**.

Their evil uncle, Amulius, was afraid that when the the twin **fratres** grew up they would try to become **rex**. While their **pater**, Mars, was away, he took the **pueri**, put them in a basket, and abandoned them in the great Tiber River. The basket floated away.

Miraculously, a **mater lupa** was drinking from the Tiber River with her **filiae** when she spotted the basket with the **pueri** inside. Even more miraculously, she plucked the basket from the Tiber and as soon as she saw the sad **fratres**. She decided to become their **mater**. The **mater lupa** gave them milk alongside her **filiae**.

When the **fratres** grew up to be young boys, the **lupa** knew she could not care for them anymore. One day, she took the **fratres** to the **domus** of a pastor. The **pastor** and his wife found the **pueri** and decided to raise them as their own children. Romulus and Remus grew up with the **pastor** and believed that the **pastor** was their **pater**.

The **pueri** grew up to be strong and clever leaders. People came to them for help settling their problems. One day, the **pastor** told him that he was not their **pater**. When they discovered who their true **pater** and **mater** were, they returned to their true **domus**. They realized that their evil uncle had become the **rex**, and they needed to take him down so that Numitor could be **rex** again. They forced the evil **rex** off the throne.

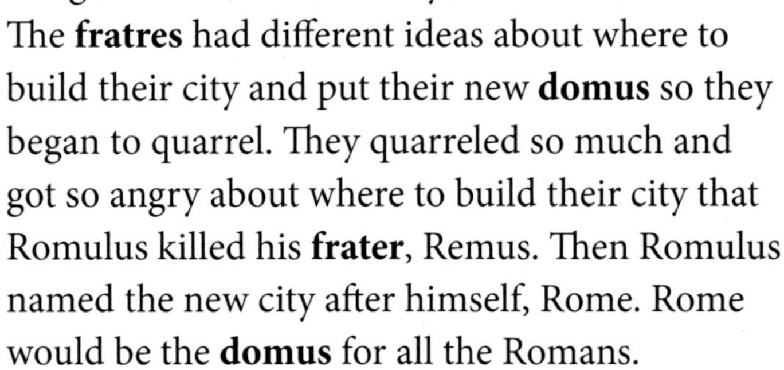

Then both the **fratres** were eager to rule and decided to leave their **domus** on Alba Longa and found a new city. The **fratres** had different ideas about where to build their city and put their new **domus** so they began to quarrel. They quarreled so much and got so angry about where to build their city that Romulus killed his **frater**, Remus. Then Romulus named the new city after himself, Rome. Rome would be the **domus** for all the Romans.

This is an important myth for Romans because it meant that their city was founded by Romulus, the son of Mars. Such a beginning meant that their city would be powerful and victorious in war.

DISCUSSION QUESTIONS

Answer the following discussion questions based on the myth of Romulus and Remus.

The myth of Romulus and Remus is about the foundation, or the beginning, of Rome. Pick a place that is important to you (for example, your city, your neighborhood, or your country). What stories do people tell about its foundation?

In the myth of Romulus and Remus the god of war, Mars, is the father of the first King of Rome. What does this tell us about how the Romans saw themselves and their city?

Does Romulus' violent solution to his conflict with Remus remind you of any other myths or historical events, ancient or modern?

Can you imagine a peaceful solution to Romulus and Remus' conflict? Write a short paragraph or skit about how the solution is reached.

Mars and Rhea Silvia, by Peter Paul Rubens

Χαῖρε!

The Greeks and Romans used myths to explain the world around them. But in order to get guidance on their everyday lives, the ancients would consult oracles. An oracle could be a person who saw the future, or an oracle could be a sign sent from the gods. The most famous of these oracles was at Delphi, the Pythia. People would travel across the world to ask her questions. In Rome, many priests practiced augury, the skill of interpreting signs from birds. In your life, where do you look when you have questions?

EXERCISE 2.3

Using your knowledge of Latin roots, answer the following questions about characters from the story of Romulus and Remus. You may wish to consult a dictionary for the italicized derivatives.

1. Who committed *fratricide*? ___________________________

2. Who tried to *domesticate* the twin brothers after they were raised in the wild? ___________________________

3. Who was not supposed to enter *matrimony*? ___________________________

4. Who wanted to steal *regal* power? ___________________________

5. Who is the *maternal* grandfather of Romulus and Remus? ___________________________

6. Who is the *paternal* grandfather of Romulus and Remus? ___________________________

7. Who could claim the *paternity* of Romulus and Remus? ___________________________

8. Though not biologically related, who is often *affiliated* with the twin babies? ___________________________

CHARACTER BANK

Rhea Silvia	Lupa, the she-wolf	Mars
Romulus	Jupiter	Numitor
Amulius	a shepherd and his wife	

ZOOM IN

In the *Harry Potter* book series by J.K. Rowling, Remus Lupin is a professor (and a werewolf) at Hogwarts, who teaches Defense Against the Dark Arts. He is named for Remus. His last name is derived from *lupus*, meaning wolf. Why do you think he was named after Remus and from the Latin word for wolf?

ADDITIONAL NOTES

ADDITIONAL NOTES

Vocabulary

LATINE	ESPAÑOL	ENGLISH
ego/me	yo/me	I/me
tu/te	tu/te	you (singular)
illud	lo/la	it
ille	el	he
illa	ella	she
nos	nosotros	we/us
vos	ustedes/vosotros	you (plural)
aqua	agua	water
caseus	queso	cheese
piscis	pescado/pez	fish
caro/carnem	carne	meat
panis	pan	bread
vinum	vino	wine
edo/comedo	como	I eat

Χαῖρε!

The Latin word *ego* is related to the Greek pronoun for I, ἐγώ. From these Latin and Greek words, we get the word "egotistical." What are some things an egotistical person might do?

LESSON 3.1: Pronouns

A **pronoun** is a word that takes the place of a _________________ often in order to make a

sentence _________________ or less _________________ .

What are some examples in Spanish or other languages that you know?

Roman family dinner

Underline the nouns in the following sentences, then rewrite the sentence using pronouns.

Minerva reads a book.

The senators give a parade to Julius Caesar.

My friends and I learn about the Romans.

In Latin, you do not always need pronouns in
a sentence, but pronouns can be used to _________________________________ who is doing an action.

ZOOM IN

In *The Hunger Games* series by Suzanne Collins, the country is called Panem. This is a form of the word *panis*. It refers to a quote by the Roman poet Juvenal, who wrote that *"panem et circenses,"* or "bread and circuses," keep common people happy. How does this quote apply to *The Hunger Games*?

Χαῖρε!

After α and β, the next letters of the Greek alphabet are gamma (γ), delta (δ), and epsilon (ε). What letters or combination of letters in our alphabet do you think these letters correspond to? Review the letters below and try writing them on your own.

Γγ Δδ Εε

EXERCISE 3.1

Choose from the items in the word bank to complete each sentence. Then translate the sentence from Latin to English.

WORD BANK

panem   caseum   carnem   piscem   aquam

1) Tu edis _____________________ .

    Anglice =

2) Nos edimus _____________________ .

    Anglice =

3) Ego edo _______________________ .

    Anglice =

4) Ille edit _____________________ .

    Anglice =

5) Vos bibitis* _____________________ .

    Anglice =

*Hint: bibitis = drink

Fish, chicken, and assorted goods

Using your food vocabulary from this chapter, can you describe what's for dinner in Latin?

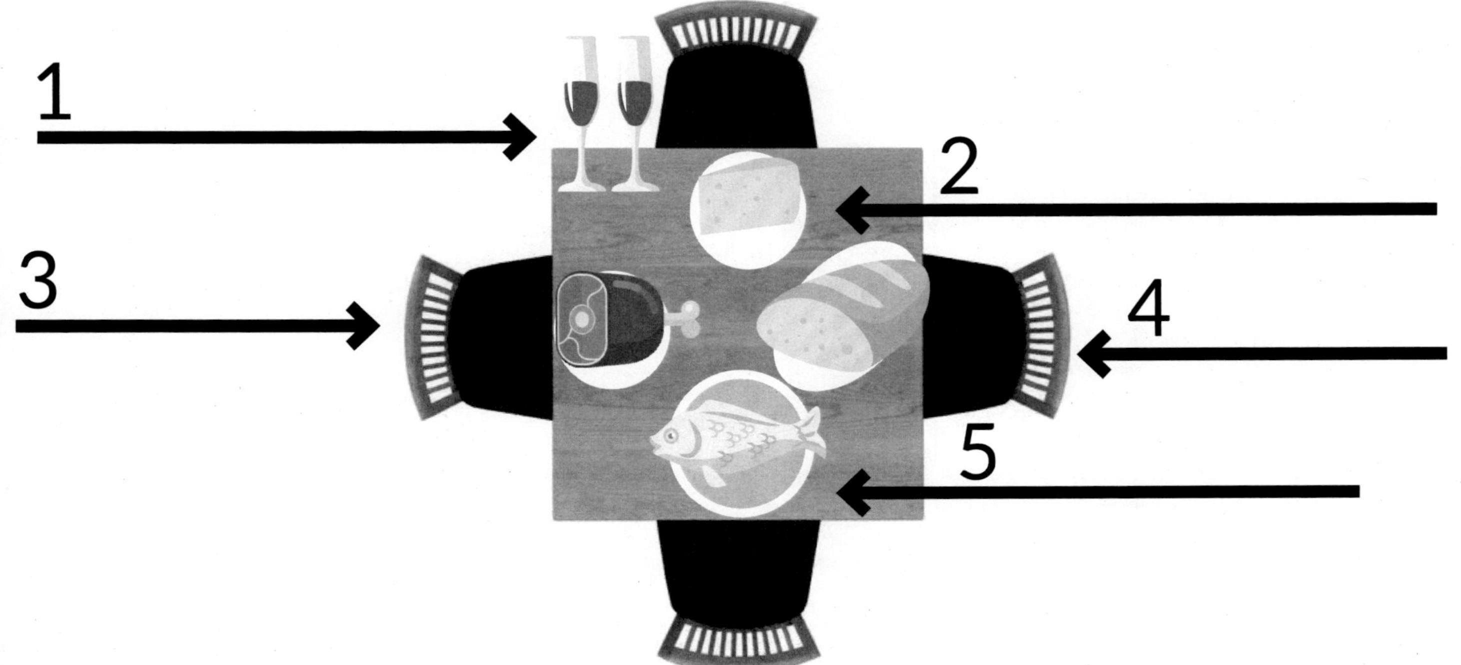

LESSON 3.2: Roman Food

There were two kinds of dinner practices for Romans, one for the middle and lower classes and one for the wealthy.

Most Roman families dined around a table on stools. The women and slaves prepared the meals, and the children served them. They typically ate

_______________________ made of vegetables and grains, but when they could afford it, they bought **panem, carnem, piscem,** and **caseum.**

The more elite Romans dined in their homes in a

_______________________ (dining room). They lounged on ___________________, leaning on their left elbow. Slaves served the food and drinks.

All Romans ate mostly with their _______________

because they did not have _______________. Sometimes they could use spoons for soups and occasionally knives to cut their food into smaller pieces to eat with their hands.

ROMAN RESTAURANTS?

This is a picture of the bar at a *popina*, a restaurant in the city that served quick food and drink, a little like a fast food restaurant today. Romans wrote about gambling, crime, and violence breaking out in these crowded ancient restaurants.

Roman food

EXERCISE 3.2

Match each English derivative with its Latin root by writing the Latin root and its meaning in the chart below. All the words are from Unit 3 vocabulary. Then, underline, circle, or highlight the letters that the roots have in common with their English derivative. The first one has been completed for you.

LATIN ROOT	ENGLISH DERIVATIVES
aqua=water	**aqu**educt
	pescatarian
	carnivore
	egotistical
	edible

In the following sentences, the bolded words are English derivatives. Using your knowledge of their Latin derivatives, what do you think these words mean?

1. Because the Romans built such a great **aqueduct** system so many years ago, the water fountains still have fresh drinking water today.
   a) Government   b) Channel carrying water   c) Postal system   d) Roads

2. My sister ordered salmon instead of a burger for dinner because she is a **pescatarian**.
   a) Someone who loves peas   b) A vegetarian
   c) Someone who does not eat any meat except fish   d) Someone allergic to cows

3. Most **carnivores** have very sharp teeth so that they can bite through raw meat.
   a) Caterpillars   b) Sharks   c) Vegetables   d) Meat-eaters

4. Emperor Commodus was so **egotistical** that he had many statues erected of him as a god.
   a) Obsessed with oneself   b) Spiritual and religious   c) Rich   d) Lonely

5. My mother's dinner was barely **edible**, so I ordered pizza instead.
   a) Hot   b) On time   c) Something you can eat   d) Poisonous plant

LESSON 3.3: Ceres and Proserpina

Read the myth about Ceres and Proserpina below. At the end of every section of the myth, there is a summary in Latin. Translate the Latin before moving on to the next section of the reading.

Ceres was the goddess of the harvest. Gods and mortals were very careful to keep Ceres happy because they knew that her moods affected all the living things in the land, including the wheat and barley that the people grew to feed themselves. The gods needed the people to harvest the grain so they would stay alive and honor the gods with sacrifices.

Ceres est dea frumenti.

____

Ceres had a daughter named Proserpina. Proserpina was a beautiful young woman, and she loved to skip through fields of flowers and collect bouquets to bring home. One day she went out to pick flowers with her friends. She wandered through the woods away from where her friends were playing.

Ceres filiam habet. Proserpina est filia Cereris.

____

____

Pluto was the king of the underworld. He was the brother of Ceres and Jupiter. He was a very unhappy god who ruled over the souls of the dead. That day he decided to drive his chariot up to the upper world for a visit. He saw the beautiful Proserpina picking flowers in the field and was dazzled by her beauty. Before Ceres could see, he grabbed Proserpina and drove his chariot down into the darkest depths of the underworld.

Pluto est rex inferorum. Ille videt Proserpinam et amat.

____

____

Pluto brought Proserpina to the underworld and made her his queen. Proserpina cried and cried. She was sad to be locked in a room in the underworld far away from her mother and the world of growing things.

WORDS TO HELP

Dea—goddess
Frumenti—of grain
Habet—has
Cereris—of Ceres
Inferorum—of the underworld
Videt—sees
Amat—loves
Regina—queen
Tristis—sad
Quaerit—looks for
Invenit—find
Ad—to
Spectat—sees/watches
Felix—happy
Filiam—daughter
Sunt—are
Felices—happy
Eunt—go
Domum—home
Omnes—everything
Florent—blooms, flourishes

Proserpina est regina inferorum. Illa est tristis.

When Ceres heard her daughter's cry, she searched for her daughter all over but could not find her. Ceres was so upset about the loss of her daughter, that she let all the crops die and a deep winter took hold of the earth.

Ceres Proserpinam quaerit. Illa Proserpinam non invenit.

Proserpina was sad in the underworld. She was eager to see her mother again and she begged to be able to return to the upper world. Seeing how unhappy she was as his queen, Pluto finally let her leave. Before bringing her back to the upper world, he offered her a pomegranate from his garden, knowing that if you eat the fruit of the underworld, you cannot return to the land of the living. Proserpina was so hungry and she ate a few seeds. Proserpina returned to the upper world and cried tears of joy when she saw her mother. Her mother cried to see her long lost daughter and held her tightly. Proserpina told her mother everything that had happened to her as her mother listened with worry. When she finished, Ceres asked anxiously, "Did you eat anything in the underworld?" She knew that anyone who ate the fruit of the underworld was doomed to remain in the underworld forever. Proserpina confessed that she had eaten six pomegranate seeds. Hearing this Ceres despaired and begged Jupiter to let her daughter stay with her. Jupiter declared that Proserpina should spend six months of every year with her mother, but would have to pass the other six months, one for each pomegranate seed, in the underworld with Pluto.

**Proserpina matrem spectat. Ceres filiam spectat.
Ceres et Proserpina sunt felices.**

Ceres and Proserpina finally returned home. The whole world rejoiced as Ceres returned to her work. The snow melted away as the sun warmed the earth. The little seeds that had lain asleep shook off the chill and peeked out of the ground. The brown grass shimmered into vibrant shades of green. Trees and flowers were relieved to bloom again with new leaves. During the six months that Ceres spent with Proserpina she again helped the people grow their crops and harvest them. But when Proserpina had to return to the underworld, Ceres again grew sad and the earth grew cold, mourning for Ceres' daughter.

Ceres et Proserpina domum eunt. Omnes florent. Omnes sunt felices.

DISCUSSION QUESTIONS

Review the myth of Ceres and Proserpina and answer the following discussion questions.

Is Proserpina treated fairly in this myth? Why or why not?

Myths often explain natural phenomena, like lightning or animal behavior— things that the Romans had trouble understanding. This myth explains why we have seasons. Think of a natural phenomenon. What are some creative ways to explain why it happens?

In Roman times, men often had more control in their choice of whom to marry and over household rules. Are there different motivations for marriage in other times and other cultures? How have things changed today?

ZOOM IN

Fluffy, the three-headed dog from *Harry Potter* by J.K. Rowling, is based on Cerberus. Cerberus guarded the underworld and also had three heads. In the series, the vicious Fluffy guards a trap door, in an area students are not allowed to go into, but he can be put to sleep by music. Similarly, Cerberus fell asleep when he heard music, allowing people to sneak into the underworld. Can you think of any other similarities between the two dogs? What is the connection between the underworld and the trap door?

Χαῖρε!

The ancients believed that, after death, people went to the underworld. Hades and Persephone were the king and queen of this domain. The Greeks and Romans believed that a soul had to pay a ferryman named Charon to take them across the river Styx and into the underworld.

EXERCISE 3.3

Can't get enough derivatives? Using the spelling and meaning of each derivative below, find its Latin root from the Words to Help box on page 33 of the Ceres and Prosperpina myth. Some Latin roots may have more than one derivative!

____________________________ 1. omnivore: animal or person who eats everything—both plants and meats

____________________________ 2. query: a question; an action done to seek an answer to something

____________________________ 3. evident: clearly seen or understood

____________________________ 4. felicity: happiness

____________________________ 5. invention: something discovered or newly created

____________________________ 6. inquire: to question or seek answers

____________________________ 7. omniscient: knowing everything

____________________________ 8. felicitous: fortunate

____________________________ 9. floral: of or relating to flowers and blossoms

____________________________ 10. visual: relating to seeing or sight

WORD	DEFINITION
Poetry	A artful form of literature typically composed according to a set structure, such as a rigid pattern of syllables or rhyme scheme
Meter	the rhythm of a poem
Syllable	A basic unit of pronunciation containing one vowel sound
Stanza	A group of lines forming a recurring unit in poetry
Rhyme	Two or more words ending with the same sound
Epic	A long poem about a heroic figure or figures
Lyric	A shorter poem about strong feelings and emotions

What do you think of when you think about poetry? Many people think that poems have to rhyme—but this is not so! Many English and Latin poems do not rhyme. Instead, these poems deploy a rhythm that repeats itself each line or sometimes each stanza. This repeated rhythm in a piece of poetry is called its meter.

Check out some examples below of English poems and songs that do not rhyme. When you read them aloud, you may find the rhythm in the words.

Shakespeare, *Julius Caesar* and *Twelfth Night*

Friends, Romans, countrymen, lend me your ears;
I come to bury Caesar, not to praise him.

If music be the food of love, play on;
Give me excess of it, that, surfeiting,
The appetite may sicken, and so die.

Robert Frost, "Mending Wall"

Something there is that doesn't love a wall.
That sends the frozen-ground-swell under it,
And spills the upper boulders in the sun...

To understand how a line of English poetry may be written with meter or rhythm, you should first understand what a syllable is. A syllable is a basic unit of pronunciation containing one vowel sound. Words may contain one or more syllables. To figure out how many syllables are in a word, you must pronounce the word out loud or in your head, not simply look at the number of letters the word contains. For example, the English word "salve" (meaning an ointment) is pronounced with one syllable because the "e" is silent, but the Latin word *salve* is pronounced with two syllables.

For a few more examples—these words all have one syllable: ***a, dog, cake, float, thought***. These words have two syllables: ***ago, apple, mother.***

Words may be pronounced with one syllable emphasized over the others. A syllable that is emphasized is said to be 'accented' whereas a syllable that is not emphasized is said to be 'unaccented'. Can you figure out which syllables are accented in the following words? Mother, apple, forgot, together, emphasize.

In English, the number of syllables per line combined with the rhythmic pattern of accented and unaccented syllables within each line gives us the meter of a poem. Looking back at the examples from Shakespeare's and Robert Frost's poetry above, what metrical patterns do you notice?

EXERCISE EL1

For the following English words, write out each syllable and underline all accented syllables:

1. cat _________________________

2. kitten _________________________

3. reading _________________________

4. poetry _________________________

5. syllable _________________________

6. pronounce _________________________

7. important _________________________

8. necessary _________________________

9. independent _________________________

10. indubitably _________________________

In Latin--and in ancient Greek too!--meter works a little differently than in English. Instead of accented and unaccented syllables, the Greeks and Romans based the rhythm of their poems on long and short syllables, in other words on how long it took them to pronounce certain vowel sounds and vowel and consonant combinations.

What precisely makes a 'long' versus a 'short' syllable in Latin? That explanation lies beyond the scope of this textbook. You'll have to keep studying Latin to find out! For now, examine the following lines of real Latin poetry. Read the Latin aloud and count the syllables. Do you notice any patterns or feel any rhythms in the Latin? A translation is provided as well, but rhythm is often lost when poems are translated to another language.

Catullus, Poem 85

Odi et amo. Quare id faciam, fortasse requiris.
Nescio, sed fieri sentio et excrucior.

I hate and I love. How do I do this, perhaps you wonder.
I don't know, but I feel it is happening and I am tortured.

Vergil, Aeneid Book I, lines 1-4

Arma virumque cano, Troiae qui primus ab oris
Italiam, fato profugus, Laviniaque venit
Litora, multum ille et terris iactatus et alto
Vi superum saevae memorem Iunonis ob iram...

Arms I sing, and the man who first, from the shores of Troy,
exiled by fate, reached Italy and the Lavinian
coast, much tossed about on sea and land by the violence
of the gods, through fierce Juno's unforgetting wrath...

Sulpicia, Poem 3, lines 1-2

Scis iter ex animo sublatum triste puellae?
natali Romae iam licet esse suo.

Do you know that the weight of such a sad journey has been
lifted from the girl's heart? Now she is allowed to be in Rome
on her birthday.

Vocabulary

LATINE	ESPAÑOL	ENGLISH
pugno, pugnare	pelear/pugnar	to fight
amo, amare	amar	to love, to like
specto, spectare	mirar	to watch
timeo, timere	temer/tener miedo	to fear, to be afraid
fugio, fugere	huir	to flee, to run away
capio, capere	coger/tomar/agarrar	to take, to seize
vinco, vincere	vencer	to conquer
miles, milites	soldado/militar	soldier, soldiers
arma	armas/armadura	weapons, armor
gladius	espada	sword
pilum	jabalina	javelin
scutum	escudo	shield

Χαῖρε!

After γ, δ, and ε, the next letters of the Greek alphabet are zeta (ζ), eta (η), and theta (θ). What letters or combination of letters in our alphabet do you think these letters correspond to? Try practicing writing the Greek letters on your own.

Ζζ Ηη Θθ

LESSON 4.1: Verbs

A **verb** is an____.

What are some examples in Spanish or other languages that you know?

There is also something called a _________________________________ **verb**, as in the sentences:

> She **is** strong. I **am** happy.

Notice that in English, verbs have different _________________ and _________________.

> For example: *cook, cooks, cooked, cooking, catch, caught*

Can you think of other examples?

Latin verbs will also have different endings and forms!

Χαῖρε!

Speaking of **timeo**, have you ever experienced claustrophobia or arachnophobia? These are our modern day words for fear of small spaces and fear of spiders. They come from the Greek word for fear, *phobos* (φόβος). What phobias do you have?

EXERCISE 4.1

Using the spelling and meaning of each derivative below, find its Latin root from the Unit 4 vocabulary list.

1. *repugnant*: **distasteful, contrary, offensive** _______________________

2. *intimidate*: **to frighten someone especially to make them do something that you want** _______________________

3. *convince*: **to persuade someone** _______________________

4. *amiable*: **friendly, likable** _______________________

5. *armadillo*: **a nocturnal mammal with a jointed protective covering made of bony plates** _______________________

6. *fugitive*: **a person who is fleeing or running away** _______________________

7. *gladiator*: **a person in ancient Rome who was armed with a sword and compelled to fight to the death** _______________________

8. *inspection*: **the act of viewing something carefully or critically** _______________________

9. *captivity*: **the state of being held imprisoned or confined** _______________________

10. *militant*: **engaged in warfare; aggressive** _______________________

LESSON 4.2: Roman Army and Imperatives

The Romans were able to conquer huge territories—beginning with Italy and extending to North Africa, Greece, the Middle East, France, Spain, Germany—because they had a large and well-organized army.

In the earliest days of the Roman Empire, Roman citizens were both farmers and soldiers who would volunteer to fight to defend their home from attack. As the city grew and the empire expanded, the Roman army became a powerful force of professional, well-trained soldiers.

One of the most famous men in history, **Gaius Julius Caesar**, gained power through his military career. During the Gallic Wars (58-50 BC), Caesar fought against various native tribes that lived in what are now called France and Belgium. After he led the Roman troops to victory, Caesar became very wealthy and politically powerful. To some **senatores**, Caesar's power was a threat, so they devised a plot to assassinate him on the Ides of March.

The Roman army was made up of groups called **legiones**. The legiones were each made up of about 4,000 to 6,000 **milites**. In battle, **milites** fought each other with **gladii** and **pila**. They spent much of their time building, setting up camp, and marching very long distances. Roman soldiers marched while carrying a huge weight of weaponry, food rations, and other supplies.

Armor was made of iron and leather, and the most common **arma** were a **gladius** and **a pilum**.

A Roman soldier would serve for 25 years. Retired soldiers received a pension and a plot of farmland. Retired soldiers were called **veterani**.

What English words do we get from *legiones*, *veterani*, and *milites*?

IMPERATIVES

Have your parents ever said, "Clean your room!" or "Do your homework!"? If so, they were using

________________________________!

An imperative is a ________________________________
form of the verb. What are some other examples of commands you might hear in English?

Unlike English, Latin uses a ________________________
form to command one person, and a plural form when you are addressing more than one person.

For some verbs, to form the imperative in Latin, you start with the **infinitive**, or the form of the verb

often ending in ____________e.g. ________________________ and drop the -re".

To form a plural imperative, you follow the same process and add __________ to the end of the word.
However, there are some exceptions to these rules!

Review this chart of imperatives.
What patterns do you notice? What commands don't follow the rules?
What ending is common in all the plural imperative forms?
How would you form the imperatives for the last two verbs that are left blank?

INFINITIVE	SINGULAR IMPERATIVE	PLURAL IMPERATIVE
salvere	salve	salvete
valere	vale	valete
pugnare	pugna	pugnate
amare	ama	amate
fugere	fuge	fugite
spectare		spectate
timere	time	

EXERCISE 4.2

Below are descriptions of Roman soldiers performing certain actions. Imagine that you are a commander in the Roman army and want to instruct people to carry out these actions. Which command would you give? Choose the correct imperative from the word bank for each description. You will not use all the words from the word bank, so be mindful of singulars and plurals!

1. **One Roman soldier running away**

2. **Two Roman soldiers arresting an enemy**

3. **One Roman soldier charges into battle**

4. **One Roman soldier gazing across the fields**

5. **Two Roman soldiers shiver with fear**

6. **Many Roman soldiers win a battle**

Label the Roman soldier with the vocabulary used from the lesson.

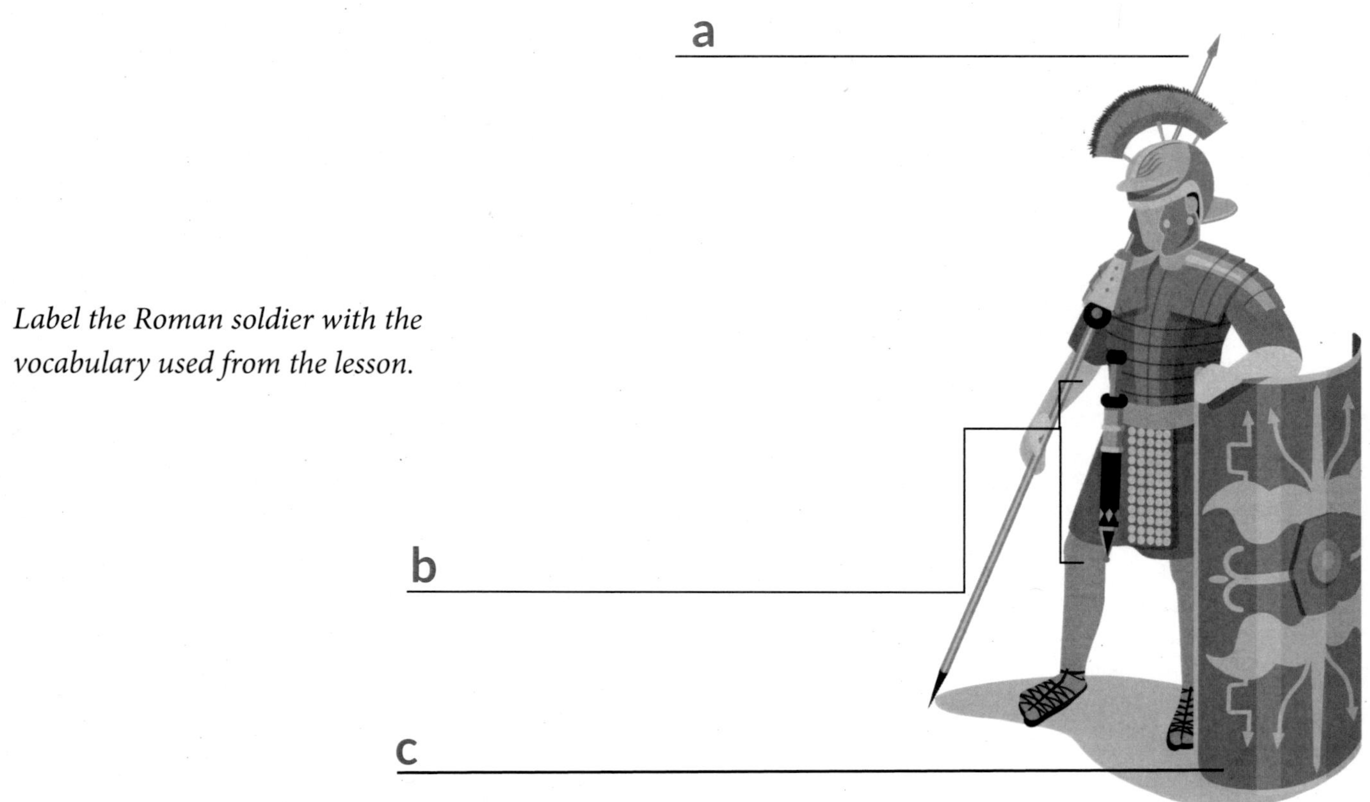

LESSON 4.3: Theseus and the Minotaur

There once was a king named Minos who lived on a beautiful Greek island called Crete. King Minos had a daughter named Ariadne, and his island was perfect except for one small detail, a giant and dangerous half-man, half-bull lived on the island and would terrify the people of Crete. King Minos decided to have a giant labyrinth , or maze, built to keep the monster hidden away.

Minos est rex Cretae. Ariadne est filia Minonis. Minos et Ariadne et Minotaurus in Creta habitant.

Minotaur

The story of the frightful Minotaur spread across the land and everyone in Greece was afraid of the monster. There was a small city across the sea from Crete named Athens, but Athens was not as strong or powerful as Crete. King Minos demanded that Athens send seven girls and seven boys every nine years to be fed to his monster.

Graeci Minotaurum timent. Minotaurus pueros et puellas edit.

Labyrinth

Theseus lived in Athens, and he decided he had to do something about the Minotaur and save his people. Theseus' father was the King of Athens, and when Theseus told his father that he was going to slay the Minotaur, his father remarked, "Oh no, my son, you cannot go to Crete to slay the Minotaur for you will surely die! Even if you are successful in defeating the giant beast, you will never find your way back out of the labyrinth!" Theseus replied, "Don't worry father! I will find a way!"

Theseus est filius regis. Theseus vult vincere Minotaurum.

Theseus sailed to Crete with the other boys and girls and was taken by King Minos. But the Cretan princess, Ariadne had never seen such a strong, handsome hero as Theseus. That night Ariadne tossed and turned, worrying about Theseus and his fate in the labyrinth, but then she had a brilliant idea! She grabbed

WORDS TO HELP

Habito, habitare—to live
Regis—of the king
Vult—wants
Linea—string
Adiuvo, adiuvare—to help
Do, dare—to give

a ball of string and ran down through the palace. She burst into Theseus' room and said, "Theseus! Take this ball of string and tie one end to a tree at the beginning of the labyrinth! Unwind the string as you walk through the maze and then you will be able to follow it out!"

Ariadne Theseum amat. Ariadne Theseum adiuvat. Ariadne lineam et gladium Theseo dat.

____

____

Theseus took the string and followed Ariadne's advice. With a little help from the gods he slew the Minotaur. No one was more excited to see him than Ariadne, and they sailed away together back to Athens.

Theseus lineam et gladium capit et Minotaurum vincit. Theseus et Ariadne Cretam fugiunt.

____

____

DISCUSSION QUESTIONS

Answer and discuss the following reading questions about the myth of the Minotaur.

How did Theseus find his way back out of the labyrinth?

Who is Theseus' father?

Where does King Minos live?

Where does Ariadne live?

Responde Latine: Would you volunteer to fight the minotaur?

What do you think makes a person a hero?

What motivates Ariadne to help Theseus? Is she heroic for helping him?

ZOOM IN

The Hunger Games series, by Suzanne Collins, is inspired by the idea of tributes from the myth of Theseus. In both stories, young men and women are selected to travel to another city. There, they face a series of tasks that almost always leads to death. Theseus volunteers to take someone's place, like Katniss in the series. What are other connections between the two stories?

Χαῖρε!

According to the Athenians, our hero Theseus eventually became the king of Athens. After ruling for a while, he decided to step down from the throne and handed the power over to the people. In doing this, Theseus founded the world's first democracy, Athens. Did you know democracy is a Greek word too? What do you think it means?

ESCAPE THE LABYRINTH!

Help Theseus thread the yarn to find his way out of the labyrinth! The black dots mark the spaces where you should cut or punch holes for threading your yarn. Tape or tie your yarn at the labyrinth entrance, then use the yarn to connect the phrase to its translation on the other side.

Labyrinth Entrance

Tu times 

spectate scutum! 

ille pugnat 

nos amamus 

fugite! 

cape gladium! 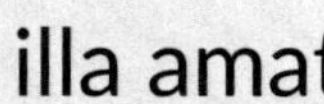

nos spectamus 

illa amat 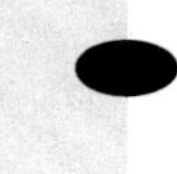

vos pugnatis 

illud timet

ego vinco

 watch the shield!

you (pl.) fight

take the sword!

she loves

you fear

we watch

he fights

it fears

I conquer

we love

Flee!

Labyrinth Exit

ADDITIONAL NOTES

EXCERCISE 4.3: MADLIBS

Now that you have learned about different parts of speech, you can plug Latin words into the skit below to make a funny scene. When a blank has (N), choose a Latin noun for the space. When it has (V), choose a Latin verb.

NOUNS
nomen, nihil, gratias, pater, mater, frater, rex, pastor, puer, puella, domus, lupus, filia, aqua, caseus, panis, caro, vinum, miles, gladius, arma (or use names of any gods/goddesses)

VERBS
edere, pugnare, amare, spectare, timere, fugere, capere, vincere

---

Jupiter: Salvete, (N) _____________________ and (N) _____________________ .

Are you going (V) _____________________ today?

Minerva: Oh my (N) _____________________ ! I was actually planning

(V)_____________________ (N) _____________________ instead.

Mars: Juno has commanded me (V) _____________________ (N) _____________________

for the entire week, so I am very busy.

Jupiter: Well, that sounds very reasonable. I bought a bunch of (N) _____________________

yesterday and would like to share it with the (N) _____________________ .

Minerva: Are you sure that's wise? The Romans are a strange (N) _____________________

and they are always trying (V) _____________________ it.

Mars: They make me so angry when they do that. I have to chew (N) _____________________

to feel better or else I will have to start another war.

Minerva: Oh dear. The last time you started a war, my pet (N) _____________________

was too frightened and ran far away from Mount Olympus.

Jupiter: Well, seems like I will have (V) _____________________(N) _____________________

all by myself after all. I will see you when the (N) _____________________

is high in the sky!

THESEUS AND THE MINOTAUR SKIT

King Minos: My name is Minos. *Mihi nomen est Minos.* I am the King of Crete. *Ego sum rex Cretae.*

Ariadne: My name is Ariadne. *Mihi nomen est Ariadne.* King Minos is my father. *Rex Minos est mihi pater.* I live in Crete. *Ego habito in Creta.* I have no friends here and I am very lonely.

King Aegeus: My name is Aegeus. *Mihi nomen est Aegeus.* I am the King of Athens. *Ego sum rex Athenarum.* Athens is across the sea from Crete.

Theseus: My name is Theseus. *Mihi nomen est Theseus.* King Aegeus is my father. *Mihi pater est rex Aegeus.* I live in Athens. *Ego habito Athenis.*

Minotaur: My name is Minotaur. *Mihi nomen est Minotaurus.* I am a minotaur. *Ego sum minotaurus.* My father is a bull. *Mihi pater est taurus.* I am part bull and part man. I live in a labyrinth. *Ego habito in labyrintho.* I have no friends in my labyrinth and I am very lonely. Everyone is afraid of me. *Omnes timent me.*

Ariadne: I am afraid of the Minotaur. *Ego timeo Minotaurum.*

Minos: I am afraid of the Minotaur. *Ego timeo Minotaurum.*

Aegeus: I am afraid of the Minotaur. *Ego timeo Minotaurum.*

Theseus: I am not afraid of the Minotaur. *Ego non timeo Minotaurum.*

Everyone except Theseus: What? You are not afraid? *Tu non times?*

Theseus: No! I will sail from Athens to Crete to conquer the Minotaur. *Ego vinco Minotaurum.*

Ariadne: Conquer the minotaur! *Vince Minotaurum!*

In this activity, you are acting out part of the story of Theseus and the Minotaur. The ancient Greeks called this art form δράμα (drama). What does our word "drama" mean today? For the Greeks, dramas included a χορός (chorus) of musicians and dancers that accompanied the play.

King Aegeus: Do not fight the Minotaur! *Noli pugnare in Minotaurum!* Flee the Minotaur! *Fuge Minotaurum!* The Minotaur is very dangerous and he is hidden in the middle of a giant labyrinth. Even if you manage to kill him, you will never find your way out of the maze! Do not fight the Minotaur! *Noli pugnare in Minotaurum!*

Theseus: Sorry, father. I have to fight the Minotaur. I will save everyone from the Minotaur.

King Minos: How? *Quomodo?*

Theseus: I don't know how yet, but I will figure it out.

Minotaur: Who? *Quis?*

Theseus: Yes, you. Get ready to fight! *Para pugnare!*

Ariadne: Wait! *Mane!*

Theseus: What? *Quid?*

Ariadne: I have a plan. Take this ball of string and this sword. Tie the string to a tree at the beginning of the Labyrinth and unroll it as you find your way through the labyrinth. You know what to do with the sword! Conquer the minotaur! *Vince Minotaurum!*

Theseus: Thanks! *Gratias!*

Theseus finds and fights the Minotaur. Theseus wins the fight and finds his way back to Ariadne.

Ariadne: You did it! Well done! *Bene!* Wonderful! *Mirabile!*

Theseus: Yes. Thank you for the string and sword. *Gratias pro linea et gladio.* Now time to sail home to see my father.

Ariadne: Bring me with you! *Fer me tecum!*

Theseus: Ok. Let's go! *Eamus!*

FINIS.

Χαῖρε!

Vocabulary

LATINE	ESPAÑOL	ENGLISH
quid	¿Qué?	what
quis	¿Quién?	who
ubi	¿Dónde?	where
quando	¿Cuándo?	when
cur	¿Por qué?	why
quantum	¿Cuánto/a?	how much
quot	¿Cuántos/as?	how many
stilus	lápiz/estilo	pen/pencil
magister, magistra	maestro, maestra	male teacher, female teacher
discipuli	alumnos/estudiantes	students
ianua	puerta	door
fenestra	ventana	window
tabula	tabla para escribir	writing slate

LESSON 5.1: Interrogatives

An interrogative introduces a __________________________________.

Can you think of some examples in English?

Do you need to have an interrogative word to ask a question?

Χαῖρε!

After ζ, η, and θ, the next letters of the Greek alphabet are iota (ι), kappa (κ), and lambda (λ). What letters or combination of letters in our alphabet do you think these letters correspond to? Practice writing iota, kappa, and lambda on your own.

Ιι   Κκ   Λλ

EXERCISE 5.1

Identify which Latin interrogative works best for the blank. Each word from the word bank may only be used once.

WORD BANK						
Quando	Quid	Quis	Ubi	Cur	Quot	Quantum

1. __________________ are you doing for the weekend?

2. __________________ is my dog?!? He's lost!

3. __________________ gods live on Mount Olympus?

4. __________________ is the sky blue?

5. __________________ was invited to Jupiter's birthday party?

6. __________________ water is in the sea?

7. __________________ does Jupiter's party start?

LESSON 5.2: Roman Education

Educatio (education) was very important to the Romans. Only wealthier children received a formal **educatio** either at school or at home with a private tutor. Generally, formal schools like ours today were only for boys and their families had to pay a small fee for them to attend.

There were three types of schools in Ancient Rome. The first type was called a **ludus** and was for boys around the ages of seven to twelve. The **ludi magister** taught them reading, writing, and basic mathematics. Older boys attended more advanced schools taught by a **grammaticus** where they learned specialized subjects, like history, literature, and Greek. There was a third level of school led by a **rhetor** for elite young men. They might be sent to Greece in order to study with the **rhetor** to practice public speaking and to discuss philosophy.

A papyrus of the Iliad, in Ancient Greek, one of the most important subjects of instruction

Fresco of a girl reading with her mother, from the villa of the Mysteries, near Pompeii

Children wrote with a **stilus** on a wax **tabula**. They went to school everyday with no break on the weekends. However, they did have many more school holidays than students today.

Most girls did not go to school publicly—instead they learned how to run a household, be a good wife, play music, and sew. Wealthier families often hired tutors for their daughters so they could receive more formal **educatio** at home, where they learned to read, write, and basics in literature and history. The poet Sulpicia is known for a collection of poems written during the time of Augustus, and Hortensia used her knowledge of Roman law and oratory to argue successfully for unfair taxes on women to be reformed.

CULTURAL CONNECTION

For centuries in Europe, people would read classical Latin texts by famous authors such as Cicero and Caesar to improve their writing style or educate themselves in philosophy and politics to prepare for public office. Similarly, in the past, young Chinese scholars would recite and memorize classic texts written in classical Chinese, whose authors include Confucius and Mencius, to become literate and prepare themselves for the Chinese bureaucracy.

EXERCISE 5.2

Match each English derivative with its Latin root by writing the Latin root and its meaning in the chart below. All the words are from Unit 5 vocabulary. Then, underline, circle, or highlight the letters that the roots have in common with their English derivative. The first one has been completed for you.

ENGLISH DERIVATIVES	LATIN ROOT
quantity	**quant**um=how much
ubiquitous	
defenestrate	
interdisciplinary	
magisterial	

In the following sentences, the underlined words are English derivatives. Using your knowledge of their Latin derivatives, what do you think these words mean?

1. We brought a huge **quantity** of food to the school picnic.
   a) Amount of something   b) Basket   c) Variety   d) Price of something

2. A **ubiquitous** symbol for love is a heart.
   a) Strange   b) Existing everywhere   c) Pretty and cute   d) Ironic

3. I will **defenestrate** you, and we are five stories up.
   a) To marry   b) To laugh
   c) To send on the elevator   d) To throw out a window

4. As a **disciple** of Pythagoras, he wanted to learn everything he could from him.
   a) Follower   b) Father   c) Doctor   d) Enemy

5. She stood in front of the class and taught the lesson looking very **magisterial**.
   a) Confused   b) Frightened of crowds
   c) Being a master or a teacher   d) Hungry

Χαῖρε!

The Greeks also thought education was very important. Their education, παιδεία (*paideia*), included subjects like gymnastics, mathematics, philosophy, dance, rhetoric, and music. Children learned songs and epic poems. Epics are long dramatic poems meant to be recited out loud. Some people memorized and recited epics that are thousands of lines long, such as *The Iliad* and *The Odyssey*. What's the longest thing you have ever memorized?

LESSON 5.3: Arachne and Minerva

Minerva was the Roman goddess of wisdom, strategy, arts, and trade. She was excellent at weaving beautiful tapestries.

Minerva est dea. Minerva texit bene.

____

____

All the Roman women prayed to Minerva to help them with their weaving work except for one young shepherd's daughter named Arachne. Legend has it that Arachne learned to spin wool and weave beautifully before she could talk. She spent all her time sitting in front of her loom making beautiful pictures with brightly colored threads.

Arachne est filia pastoris. Arachne texit bene.

____

____

Arachne's family was so proud of her work, and they took her to competitions to show off her skills. Every contest that she entered, she won. She began to think that she was the best weaver in the whole land. When she won even more contests she thought she was the best weaver that ever lived. She stopped praying and sacrificing to Minerva and began to think that her skills were due to her own hard work alone. She believed that the student had surpassed the master.

Quot certamina lanifica Arachne vincit? Cur Arachne non adorat Minervam?

> ### WORDS TO HELP
> **texo, texere**—to weave
> **pastoris**—of a shepherd
> **certamina**—contests, competitions
> **lanifica**—weaving
> **adoro, adorare**—to worship, honor
> **irata**—angry
> **mutat**—changes
> **aranea**—spider

____

____

At one competition an old woman overhead her boasts and challenged her, saying, "You are not the best weaver in the world. Don't you know that Minerva is better than any mortal?" "No," Arachne replied, "I am the best weaver there ever was and ever will be." At that moment the old woman transformed into a tall, beautiful goddess, and Arachne realized that she was speaking with Minerva herself.

Arachne: "Minerva non texit optime! Ego texo optime!"

____

____

Minerva challenged Arachne to a weaving competition, and they began to weave straight away. Minerva's tapestry was a beautiful picture of Jupiter and Juno punishing mortal men and women who challenged the gods. Arachne's tapestry depicted the gods' worst behaviors, and her skills did rival Minerva's own. When Minerva looked at the tapestry she was shocked to see how good it was, perhaps even better than her own! She was so angry with Arachne that she ripped her tapestry off of the loom's frame and tore it to pieces. Then turning to the shepherd's daughter, she cursed her to weave forever and turned her into a spider.

Dea et puella sunt in certamine. Minerva et Arachne texunt. Puella texit bene. Dea irata est. Minerva mutat puellam. Arachne est aranea.

____

____

____

DISCUSSION QUESTIONS

How would you describe Minerva's personality in this myth? Arachne's?

Do you think Arachne's punishment was fair? Why or why not?

When is competition a good thing? When is it problematic?

Χαῖρε!

Arachne's name is itself a hint about her fate at the end of our myth. Arachne (ἀράχνη) is the ancient Greek word for spider. It is also related to the Spanish word for spider, _araña_. What does the word arachnophobia mean?

EXERCISE 5.3

Use the suggested Latin sentences to match with the answer to the following Latin questions.

________ 1. Quis est Minerva?   A. Arachne est discipula Minervae.

________ 2. Quis est Arachne?   B. Arachne discit lanificium.

________ 3. Quid discit Arachne?   C. Arachne est filia pastoris.

________ 4. Quis est pater Arachnes?   D. Minerva est dea lanificii et sapientiae.

Answer the following reading comprehension questions in English.

1. **Cur** does Minerva transform Arachne into a spider?

2. **Quot** contests does Arachne win?

3. **Quis** is Arachne's teacher?

4. **Ubi** do spiders live?

5. **Quid** does Arachne depict in her tapestry?

ADDITIONAL NOTES

Vocabulary

LATINE	ESPAÑOL	ENGLISH
laetus/a	feliz/ledo	happy
iratus/a	enojado/a	angry
validus/a	valente, fuerte	strong, brave
miser/a	triste, miserable, desdichado/a	sad, miserable, wretched
fortunatus/a	afortunado/a	lucky, fortunate
bellus/a	bello/a	pretty, handsome
novus/a	nuevo/a	new
fatigatus/a	cansado, fatigado/a	tired
mortuus/a	muerto/a	dead
magnus/a	grande	big, great

Χαῖρε!

After ι, κ, and λ, the next letters of the Greek alphabet are mu (μ) and nu (ν). What letters or combination of letters in our alphabet do you think these letters correspond to? Practice writing mu and nu on your own.

LESSON 6.1: Adjectives

An **adjective** describes a _________________________________ .

Can you think of some examples in English?

In languages like Latin and Spanish, nouns, pronouns, and adjectives are assigned a

____ The most common genders are:

_____________________ __________________________ __________________________

You can usually tell what gender a word is by looking at its _______________________________.
One really common masculine ending in Latin is "-us." A really common feminine
ending in Latin is "-a." Similarly, a really common neuter ending in Latin is "-um." There
is often no logical reason for a word's gender — it
simply is what it is. Take *fenestra*, which means
"window," for example. It ends in the feminine
ending "-a" but there is no good reason for it to be feminine
instead of masculine or neuter. Other times, though, a word's
gender is what we expect it to be. For example, *avus* means
"grandfather" and its gender is masculine.

In Spanish, there is no such thing as "neuter," like in Latin, so all
Spanish words are either "*masculino*" or "*feminino*." Similar to
Latin, however, the gender of words may either correspond to
our expectations or be arbitrarily assigned. For example, *mujer*
means "woman" and is *feminino*. Likewise, *hombre* means "man"
and is *masculino*. However, we would not expect an object, like
mesa ("table"), to have a gender and yet it is
feminino (*la mesa*).

In Latin, masculine adjectives end in _____________________ .

In Latin, feminine adjectives end in _____________________ .

Χαῖρε!

What are your favorite colors to wear? Many people assume that the Romans and Greeks wore
white togas all the time, when in reality, they wore a variety of garments adorned in bright reds,
greens, blues, and yellows. Several words for color in Spanish come from Latin, such as *verde*
from *viridis*. What does verde mean in English?

EXERCISE 6.1

Choose 8 of the 12 different types of people below. Write the name of each and a Latin adjective to describe them.

PERSON TYPE	NAME	LATIN ADJECTIVE
1. a family relative		
2. a pet		
3. a celebrity		
4. a friend		
5. a character from a book		
6. a cartoon character		
7. yourself		
8. a character from a TV show or movie		
9. a mythological character		
10. an athlete		
11. an historical figure		
12. an author		

Below are Latin nouns you have already learned with adjectives from this lesson. What do you think the ending for each of the adjectives below should be so that they match their nouns in grammatical gender?

1. **Aqua bell________**

2. **Exercitus valid_______**

3. **Discipulus laet_______**

4. **Fenestra magn_______**

5. **Lupus irat_______**

6. **Filia fortunat_______**

"

LESSON 6.2: Roman Clothing

Roman clothing was made of wool, silk, cotton, and leather. The most common form of clothing was the belted _______________________________.

Adult male citizens were allowed to wear a _______________________________, which was a long piece of fabric draped around the shoulders. **Togae** were usually only worn for special occasions. Women wore a (dress)

_______________________, which was held together by _______________________ (buckles) and buttons, and a _______________________ (shawl/coat).

Young boys usually wore a **tunica** and a _______________________ (locket or amulet) until around sixteen years old when they transitioned to wearing the

____

(the toga of manhood).

Young girls also wore a **tunica**, but they wore their **bulla** until they were

_______________________________________. The bulla could be made of metal or gold for wealthy Romans, or a simple cloth pouch—but either type would be filled with secret charms to protect the child from harm.

Shoes were not very different between men and women. Most Romans wore shoes that tied around the ankles with thin strips of leather. However, Romans did have shoes that were appropriate to wear

outdoors,_______________________which were a mix between a shoe and a sandal, and shoes that were appropriate to wear indoors,

_______________________________, which were sandals.

...lae _to protect children from harm._

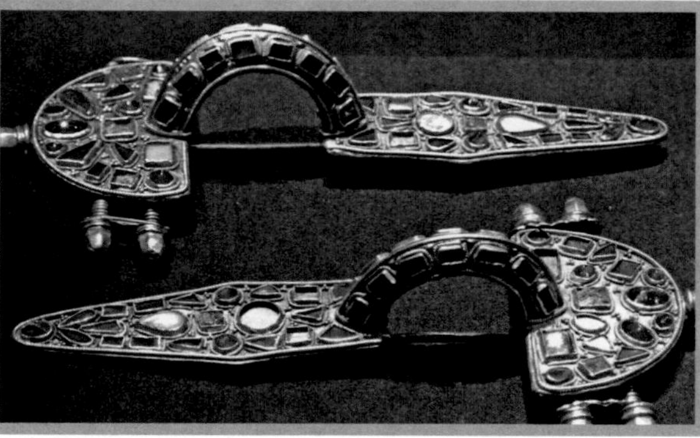

Fibulae _decorated with colorful stones._

Calcei - _Roman shoes_

EXCERCISE 6.2

Using one Roman clothing term and one adjective, describe each of the items below.

For example, a = magna toga   Remember to change the ending of your adjective to match the gender of the noun!

<table>
<tr><td colspan="2">WORD BANK</td></tr>
<tr><td>ROMAN CLOTHING</td><td>ADJECTIVES</td></tr>
</table>

WORD BANK

ROMAN CLOTHING

Toga	Stola	Fibulae	Calcei
Soleae		Bulla	Palla

ADJECTIVES

magnus	novus	fortunatus
miser/a	bellus	parvus (small)
	validus	

WHAT TO WEAR

This man is wearing a **bulla**. Although boys would remove their **bullae** when they turned sixteen years old, they might wear them again for a special occasion, like a triumphal parade, when they might attract more attention and possibly negative reactions. The **bulla** was like a lucky and protective charm to shield them from harm, malicious feelings like jealousy, or even curses.

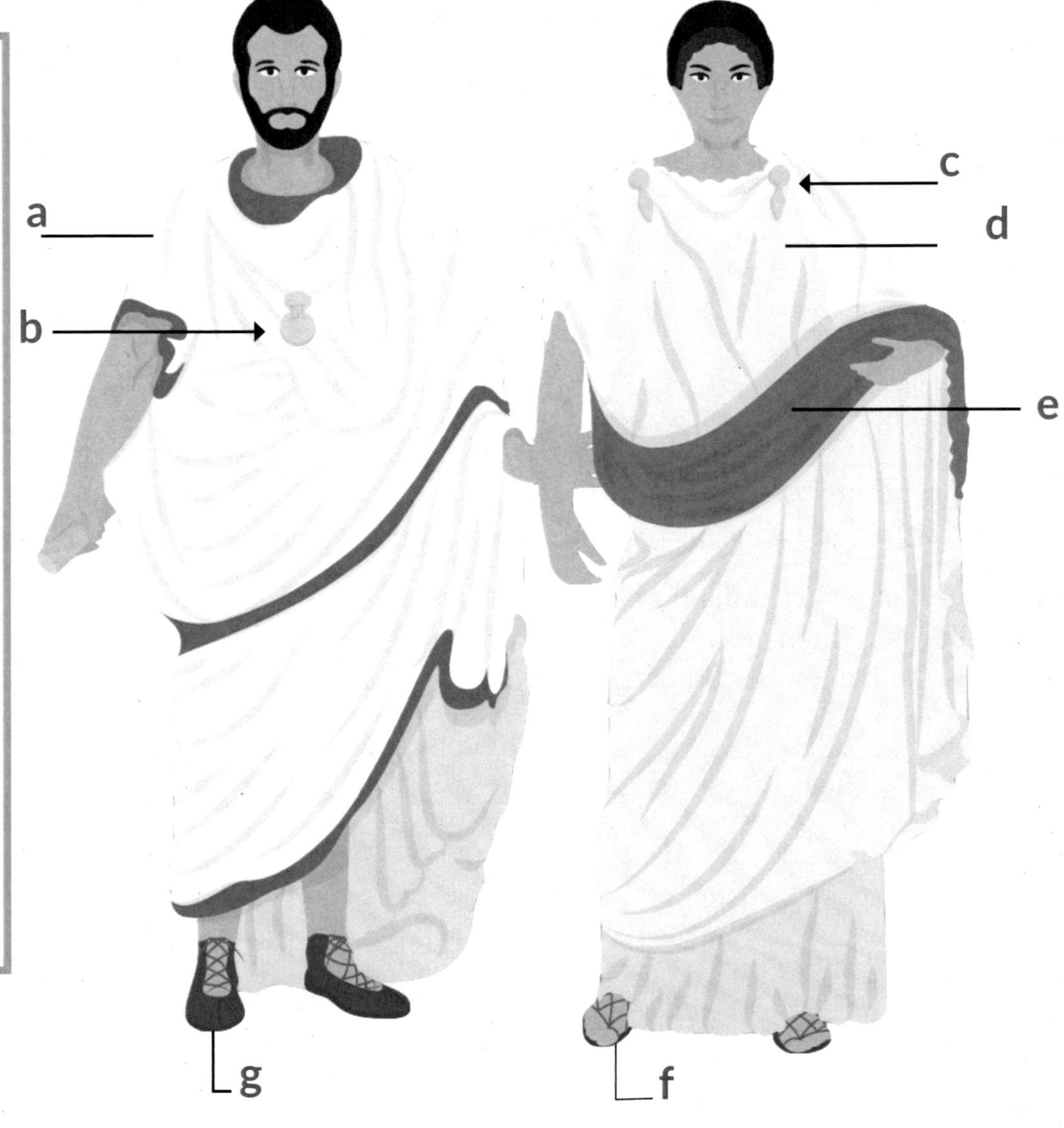

a______________________________________

b______________________________________

c______________________________________

d______________________________________

e______________________________________

f______________________________________

g______________________________________

LESSON 6.3: Echo and Narcissus

WORD BANK

bellus/bella—beautiful	parvus/parva—little	sonorus/sonora—loud
tacitus/tacita—silent	solus/sola—alone	serenus/serena—tranquil
placidus/placida—peaceful	frigidus/frigida—cold	famelicus/famelica—hungry
sitiens/sitiens—thirsty	magnus/magna—much	iratus/irata—angry
mortuus/a—dead	laetus/laeta—happy	miser/misera—miserable

Choose a Latin adjective from the word bank for each blank. Be sure to use the correct ending depending on whether the noun is feminine (f) or masculine (m).

There was once a ___________________ (f) nymph named Echo who was known for her love of talking, singing and gossiping. Echo was wandering the woods when she came upon Jupiter hanging out with other nymphs. ___________________(f) Echo knew that Juno was searching for her ___________________(m) husband Jupiter and would not be happy to find him there.

Jupiter asked Echo to distract his wife and who could refuse ___________________ (m) Jupiter's requests? Not Echo! So, Echo went to chat with Juno until finally Juno realized that Echo was trying to distract her! Juno was so ___________________ (f) that she took away most of Echo's voice, leaving her with only the ability to mimic a sound she heard.

Juno left Echo in a very ___________________(m) state. What was Echo to do without her voice?

Then Echo noticed the most ___________________ (m) boy she had ever seen, Narcissus. Narcissus wandered away from his friends through the ___________________(f) woods. Echo fell in love with him instantly and followed him, but hid behind trees and bushes because she was ashamed of her inability to talk on her own. Echo longed to call out to Narcissus , but remained silent until he realized he had lost his friends. He called out, "Is anyone here?" "Here," replied Echo from behind a bush. Narcissus was astonished to hear a ___________________(f) voice without seeing anyone around and shouted "Come to me!" "Come to me!" Echo echoed. Since no one appeared he asked, "Why are you hiding from me?" And again she asked, "Why are you hiding from me?"

Finally, he stood still and called "Here, let's meet together." "Together!" Echo exclaimed as she burst from the woods and flung her arms around him. But seeing ______________________(f) Echo,

Narcissus jumped back and shouted at her, " Don't touch me! I'd rather die than let you have my heart." And Echo answered sadly, "You have my heart!"

After this, Echo was very ______________________ (f). She wandered the woods, hiding her face in the leaves of the trees and in caves. She was so sad, her body vanished into the air. All that remains is her voice, which you can still hear her when you visit a cave or cliff.

Narcissus also met a ______________________(m) end. He wandered through the woods until he got thirsty and stopped to drink some water from a ______________________(f) pool. As he bent down to drink the ______________________ (f) water, he caught a glimpse of his reflection and was stunned by his own beauty. As time passed, he fell more and more in love with himself. He hung over the water for the entire day, then a week, a month, a year, without eating or drinking! He was very______________________ (m) and ______________________(m) but his love prevented him from leaving. Narcissus was nearly ______________________ (m) when Jupiter passed by and took pity on him, turning him into a white flower bending over the water.

CULTURAL CONNECTION

In Mexico, there is an Aztec myth that explains the existence of two major volcanoes, Iztaccíhuatl and Popocatepetl. The Aztecs were a powerful people possessing a vast empire (c. 1342—1521 CE) that dominated the majority of the Valley of Mexico.

The myth of Iztaccíhuatl and Popocatepetl takes place when the Aztecs were waging war against one of their fiercest enemies. The Aztec princess, Iztaccíhuatl, was the most beautiful in all the land and she had fallen in love with Popocatepetl, a handsome and strong warrior. Before being sent to war, Popocatepetl asked for Iztaccíhuatl's hand in marriage. Her father promised Popocatepetl that he would welcome him back with a huge engagement party if he returned victorious from war. So Popocatepetl left. While he was away, one of his jealous rivals lied to Iztaccíhuatl, saying that Popocatepetl had died in battle. Heartbroken and distraught, Iztaccíhuatl died of sadness. When Popocatepetl returned, he heard of his princess' tragic fate. In order to honor her, he ordered that a tomb be built as close to the sun as possible by piling ten hills together to make a huge mountain. Popocatepetl took his love to the top of the mountain and lay her to rest there, staying beside her with a torch. Eventually, snow covered both their bodies and formed two volcanoes that would be joined together eternally.

Χαῖρε!

Narcissus is believed to be the son of a Greek river god and a nymph. Some say the myth derives from the ancient Greek superstition that seeing one's own reflection was unlucky (or even deadly!). Can you think of any other myths that warn you against doing something? These stories are sometimes called "fables" in English, which comes from a Latin word we've seen before.

DISCUSSION QUESTIONS

Answer and discuss the following questions about the myth of Echo and Narcissus.

How did Echo lose her voice?

Why was Juno mad at Jupiter?

Who did Narcissus love?

How do you think Echo feels about her situation? How would you feel if you were Echo?

What does it mean to be a narcissist? What is a Latin derivative that we've discussed that is similar?

What is the difference between self-esteem and narcissism?

Can you think of any other story that warns you against doing something?

This story, like the story of Ceres and Proserpina, explains two natural phenomena—what are they?

DECORATIVE DESCRIPTIONS

Use the Narcissus flower and Echo accordian shapes from the materials to make foldable flaps that describe the characters from the myth. Write adjectives from the story that could describe Echo onto the blanks in her shape, and adjectives that decribe Narcissus on the blanks in his flower petals. Be sure to check that you have used the correct adjective endings! Cut both shapes out. Paste the images of Narcissus and Echo onto their respective shapes in your workbook. Fold along the dotted lines.

Paste the base part of Echo's shape here.

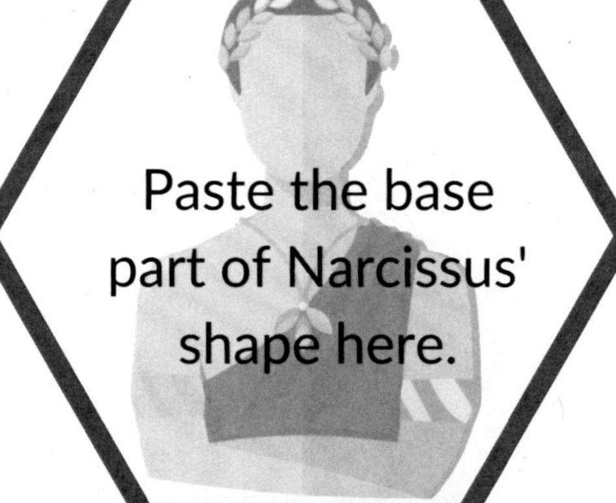

Paste the base part of Narcissus' shape here.

EXERCISE 6.3

Match each English derivative with its Latin root by writing the Latin root and its meaning in the chart below. All the words are from Unit 6 vocabulary. Then, underline, circle, or highlight the letters that the roots have in common with their English derivative. The first one has been completed for you.

ENGLISH DERIVATIVES	LATIN ROOT
mortuary	mortuus= dead
novel	
fortunately	
embellished	
magnitude	

In the following sentences, the bold words are English derivatives. Using your knowledge of their Latin roots, what do you think these words mean?

1. They died and were taken across town to the **mortuary**.
   a) Cafeteria   b) Building for dead bodies   c) Playground   d) Abandoned building

2. My sister always finds **novel** ways to reuse broken electronics.
   a) New   b) Useless   c) Scary   d) Evil

3. **Fortunately** my brother did not find the candy I hid in my sock drawer.
   a) Sadly   b) Luckily   c) Quickly   d) Quietly

4. My dad **embellished** my old dress, and I felt so pretty when I wore it.
   a) To cut up   b) To wash thoroughly   c) To trade for something new
   d) To beautify by adding details

5. Because of the **magnitude** of the project, we had to hire more workers.
   a) Difficulty   b) Budget   c) Large size   d) Success

ZOOM IN

From the myth of Narcissus, we get the word narcissistic, meaning self-centered or vain. The *Harry Potter* character Narcissa Malfoy gets her name from the same root. She allies with Voldemort and is proud of being a "pure-blood." Why do you think she was given this name?

ADDITIONAL NOTES

ADDITIONAL NOTES

UNIT 7

Vocabulary

LATINE	ESPAÑOL	ENGLISH
nunc	ahora	now
semper	siempre	always
numquam	nunca	never
lente	lentamente	slowly
celeriter	rápidamente/con celeridad	quickly
ferociter	ferozmente	fiercely
iterum	de nuevo, otra vez	again
diu	por un largo tiempo	for a long time
breviter	por un corto tiempo/en breve	for a short time
suaviter	suavemente, dulcemente	sweetly, pleasantly

Χαῖρε!

After μ and ν, the next letters of the Greek alphabet are xi (ξ) and omicron (o). What letters or combination of letters in our alphabet do you think these letters correspond to? Practice writing xi and omicron on your own.

LESSON 7.1: Adverbs

An **adverb** describes a _______________________, showing:

____________an action is done, in what _________________________, or to what _______________________

Can you think of some examples?

Adverbs can also be used to describe _______________________________ or other ___________________________.

Example: I am _ridiculously_ **handsome. He spoke** _very_ **loudly.**

In English, a common adverb ending is _________, as in _____________________ .

In Latin, common adverb endings are _________ and _________, as in ___________ and _______________________.

Look at the list of adverbs in your Unit 7 vocabulary. Which English and Latin words have the common endings? Which do not?

EXERCISE 7.1

Choose a Latin adverb for each blank below. Then read and translate your sentence.

WORD BANK					
nunc	numquam	celeriter	ferociter	breviter	pessime
semper	lente	diu	iterum	suaviter	bene

1. Ego _______________ edo carnem. Translate:

2. Rex _______________ spectat fenestram. Translate:

3. Magnus miles _________________ timet te. Translate:

4. Nos _________________ capimus novum stilum. Translate:

5. Iratus lupus _____________________ fugit gladium. Translate:

SPINNING SENTENCES

Adverbs can describe adjectives as well as verbs! Attach your golden apple spinner from materials with a metal brad fastener. Spin the apple to match an adverb with an adjective and then fill in the blanks below to create a Latin sentence.

Be sure to change your adjective endings to match the person being described, but Latin adverbs don't need any changes! Translate your sentences in the space provided.

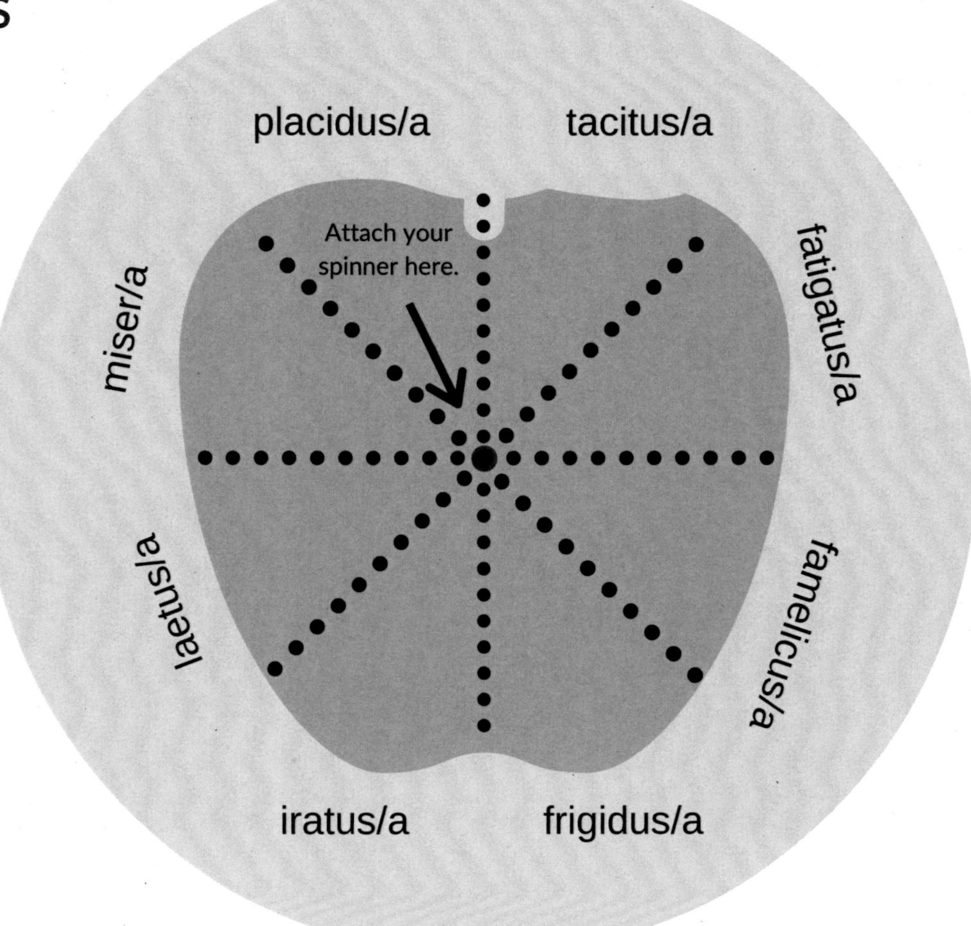

LATIN	TRANSLATION
Ego __________ __________ sum. (adverb) (adjective)	
Tu __________ __________ es. (adverb) (adjective)	
Atalanta __________ __________ est. (adjective) (adverb)	
Hippomenes __________ __________ est. (adjective) (adverb)	
Nos __________ __________ sumus (adverb) (adjective)	
Malum __________ __________ est. (adjective) (adverb)	

LESSON 7.2: Gladiators

The most famous amphitheater in Rome is called the

____

and you can still visit it today.

There, they held gladiatorial games, a popular bloody sport in the Roman Republic and Roman Empire. During the games, gladiators (or, in Latin, **gladiatores**) would fight each other in an arena, sometimes to the death, in front of a crowd of **spectatores**. Some free Romans signed up to be **gladiatores** in the hope of gaining

_______________________ and _______________________, but many **gladiatores** were

_______________________ ,

_______________________ ,

and _______________________ who were forced to fight. The very best **gladiatores** could become very rich and famous, like modern celebrities.

ZOOM IN

The movie _Gladiator_ takes us back to the time of fights to the death in the Colosseum. Maximus is the main character, played by Russell Crowe. A former general, he is sold into slavery and slowly rises to prominence as a gladiator. Eventually, he fights before the Emperor in the Colosseum, and finally takes his revenge. This movie was extremely popular when it was released. Why do you think the idea of gladiators appeals to us so much?

Gladiatores were trained in gladiatorial schools to use both wooden **gladii** and other **arma**. Some **gladiatores** fought with **gladii** and **scuta**, and others fought with

______________________ and ______________________.
Sometimes **gladiatores** fought

____

instead of other **gladiatores**.

Gladiatores fought in an ______________________________
in front of excited crowds. The amphitheater was an
arena surrounded by seats on all sides, like a modern day
football stadium. The crowds in the seats would cheer for
their favorite fighters. **Gladiatores** did not always have to fight to the death, and sometimes the fight
could be a draw. If a gladiator was not killed in combat, the

______________________________________or the ______________________________ could vote to
decide whether or not a gladiator should be killed.

Although gladiatorial games were popular, some Romans, including famous philosophers and
politicans, did not like the games and spoke out against them.

**How are gladiatorial fights similar to sports competitions today?
How are they different?**

CULTURAL CONNECTION

Bullfighting, or *corridas de toro*, is a popular event in Spanish-speaking countries
today. Much like gladiatorial sports with wild animals, these fights take place in front
of an audience and can be dangerous and violent. The matador, a person trained in
bullfighting, stands in the middle of an arena and carries a red cape which he uses to
attract and anger the bull. As the matador shows the bull the color red, the bull gets
angry and runs towards him, and the matador dodges the charging animal to avoid
getting poked by its horns.

**Las corridas de toro son eventos populares en los países hispanos. El matador, la
persona quien pelea contra el toro, se para en el medio de una arena con una capa
roja y trata de atraer la atención del toro. Cuando el matador tiene su atención, el toro
corre al matador y el matador se quita de su camino.**

EXERCISE 7.2

Match each English derivative with its Latin root by writing the Latin root and its meaning in the chart below. All the words are from Unit 7 vocabulary. Then, underline, circle, or highlight the letters that the roots have in common with their English derivative. The first one has been completed for you.

ENGLISH DERIVATIVES	LATIN ROOT
celerity	**celerit**er=swiftly
ferocity	
abbreviate	
assuage	

*In the following sentences, the **bold** words are English derivatives. Using your knowledge of their Latin roots, what do you think these words mean?*

1. At the Olympics, the spectators were amazed at the **celerity** of the runner, Usain Bolt.

   a) Food service   b) Quickness   c) Humor   d) Legs

2. The gladiators fought with such **ferocity** that the crowd cheered more loudly than ever before.

   a) Fierceness   b) Beauty   c) Large size   d) Laziness

3. It is much simpler to **abbreviate** "as soon as possible" to "ASAP."

   a) To write down   b) To shorten   c) To text   d) To paint

4. To **assuage** the angry customer, I gave him a free hamburger.

   a) To poison   b) To feed   c) To make someone cry

   d) To make someone feel better

Χαῖρε!

ADDITIONAL NOTES

Choose a Latin adverb for each blank to complete the story.

WORD BANK

semper—always   celeriter—swiftly   care—dearly   ferociter—bravely

numquam—never   tandem—finallynunc—now   facile—easily

aperte—clearly   valide—powerfully   benigne—kindly   diu—for a long time

subito—suddenly   iterum = again

Once there was a princess named Atalanta. Atalanta was very famous not only for her beauty but also because she was the best huntress, next to the goddess Diana that is. When Atalanta was a young girl she would

1_______________________ run through the woods with her hunting

dogs. One day she came across the goddess Diana and her nymphs. Diana

saw how 2_______________________ Atalanta ran and was so impressed

that she blessed Atalanta with the power to be the swiftest runner in the

whole world.

Atalanta loved Diana 3_______________________ and wanted to be

just like her. She wanted to run through the woods with her hounds, hunt

all the wild animals and 4_______________________ marry. When

Atalanta came of age to be married, she made a deal with her father, King

Schoeneus. Speaking 5_______________________ she told him that she would get married, but only

if he could find someone who could beat her in a foot race. Men came from near and far to race with

the beautiful and swift-footed Atalanta, but many years passed before anyone could even come close

to her speed and skill. Hippomenes had heard of Atalanta's beauty, hunting prowess, and incredible

speed for many years and 6_______________________ decided that 7_______________________ was

the time to see the maiden. He came to Atalanta's homeland, and indeed the moment he saw Atalanta

run he 8_______________________ fell in love with her. Hippomenes was a great athlete himself

and could 9_______________________ outrun anyone he knew. When he saw Atalanta run, however,

he knew he would never outrace her. He prayed 10_______________________ to Venus, the goddess

of love, to help him win over Atalanta. Venus smiled **11**_______________________ as she heard his prayer and took pity on Hippomenes. She gave him three golden apples along with a clever plan.

As Hippomenes raced Atalanta, she noted that he was not only very handsome but could run rather **12**_______________________ himself. They both **13**_______________________outraced their hounds, and Atalanta was a little sad to pull **14**_______________________ into the lead as they rounded the first bend. Just as she left Hippomenes, he **15**_______________________ threw the first golden apple far off the course. Atalanta could not resist the challenge and **16**_______________________ ran to catch it before returning to the track and once again overtaking Hippomenes. She **17**_______________________ surpassed him until he threw the second apple, and off she went **18**_______________________ . Just as they rounded the final bend, Hippomenes threw the final apple and prayed to Venus **19**_______________________ to grant him the strength to win the race. Atalanta bounded after the apple, catching it before it even touched the ground when **20**_______________________ Venus made the apple as heavy as an anchor. Despite her speed Atalanta realized she would **21**_______________________make it to the finish line before Hippomenes, but due to his speed, cleverness, and beauty, she was not too upset about the match!

Χαῖρε!

When Atalanta was young, her father abandoned her in the woods. After Atalanta was found and nursed by a bear, she grew up learning to hunt and fight, becoming well-known for her speed and skill. When Artemis sent a giant boar to ravage the Calydonian countryside, Atalanta was the first to wound the boar. Some say she was the only woman to join Jason and the Argonauts to retrieve the Golden Fleece. What modern heroines does Atalanta remind you of?

DISCUSSION QUESTIONS

Atalanta admired the goddess Diana. Name some of the qualities that she admired. Do you have a personal hero? What qualities do you admire in that person?

What did Venus give to Hippomenes to help him in the race?

What do you think were some motivations for Atalanta to gather the golden apples when she could have ignored them and won the race? For each motivation that you can brainstorm, list a time in your life when a similar reason motivated you.

EXERCISE 7.3 MADLIBS

Now that you have learned about different parts of speech, you can plug Latin words into the skit below to make a funny scene. When a blank has (N), choose a Latin noun for the space. When it has (V), choose a Latin verb.

NOUNS	mater, domus, lupus, rex, gladius, pastor, scutum, vinum, piscis, aqua, miles (or any gods/goddesses)
VERBS	amare, edere, videre, dicere, timere, invenire, vincere, pugnare, capere, florere
ADJECTIVES	laetus/a, iratus/a, valdus/a, miser/a, fortunatus/a, bellus/a, novus/a, fatigatus/a, mortuus/a
ADVERBS	semper, numquam, aperte, subito, celeriter, tandem, valde, care, nunc, benigne, ferociter, facile, diu, suaviter, iterum, lente

Teacher: Salvete discipuli, please_________________ (ADV) take out your _________________ (N), because today we are going to _________________ (V). If you _________________ (ADV) put _________________ (N), _________________ (N), _________________ (N) in your _________________ (ADJ) backpack you should be prepared for the day's activity. Is there anything _________________ (ADJ) that you _________________ (V) today?

Student: This weekend I _________________ (ADV) _________________ (V) my _________________ (N) and it caught on fire!

Student: This weekend I _________________ (V) in the _________________ (ADJ) park.

Teacher: Well, discipuli, gratias vobis ago for sharing this _________________ (ADJ) _________________ (N) with us. Eheu! That is all the time we have for today. Valete!!

Logos

Logos is a persuasive strategy that uses logic to convince you to agree with something. Notice that logos sounds like the English word logic. For example, if someone says to you, "Buy cookies at my store and not at the next store because mine cost less money," you will probably buy cookies at the store with the less expensive option. That's because the vendor formulated a logical, rational argument to convince you.

Ethos

Ethos is a persuasive strategy that emphasizes the believability, authority, and character of the speaker in order to convince you to support their argument. Notice how "ethos" looks like the English word "ethics" which refers to ideas of right and wrong. If someone is an expert in the topic they are trying to convince you to support, you will most likely believe their argument because of their expertise. For example, if you are sick and your friend says she knows you have the flu, you will still want to go to the doctor because they are the expert and therefore you know you can trust the doctor's diagnosis. Let's take another example, using the competing cookie stores from above. If an expert baker writes a review about the cookies from both stores and says that one is better than the other, you would buy cookies from the place that the baker says has the best cookies.

Pathos

Pathos is a persuasive strategy that appeals to one's emotions to convince them of something. We get words like "sympathy" and "empathy" from the word "pathos." For example, many commercials for animal shelters employ these strategies to get you to adopt their animals. By showing pictures of injured dogs and cats, the shelter appeals to your emotions, making you feel so attached to these animals that you will want to rescue them. If the cookie store said that buying their cookies would support a local charity or advertises other positive values, you may choose to buy their cookies because of your emotional response.

ethos, pathos, and logos all come from these Greek words: ἦθος, πάθος, λόγος

Roman Oratory

We still have many speeches that were written
and delivered by Roman orators. One of the
most famous orators was Cicero, who wrote
about political and philosophical ideas. In
ancient Rome, orators would speak at the
rostra, a podium with the prows of defeated
enemy ships attached. The rostra in the
Roman forum was made up of the six rams on
the bows of six warships that were captured
during the battle of Antium in 338 BCE.

ROSTRA

ORATION 1: Marcus Tullius Cicero, Against Catiline

Now we will read an excerpt from Cicero's first oration against Catiline. In this speech, Cicero is
trying to convince the Roman Senate that Catiline is plotting to overthrow the government and
Cicero's own power as Consul.

> "What an age, what customs! The senate is aware of all this, and the consul sees what
> is happening; yet this man is still alive. Alive! He even comes into the senate, and
> takes part in public debates. He observes each and every one of us and, with his eyes,
> he marks us out to be slain. We, however, heroic men, think that we are sufficiently
> safeguarding the state's interest if we avoid his frenzy and his violence."

Do you see any examples of ethos, pathos, or logos?

EXERCISE EL2:

*Imagine that you are trying to persuade someone to do something. Describe how you might use logos, ethos, and
pathos to convince them. (Refer to the cookie store examples above if you need help.)*

1. Persuade someone to quit smoking.
2. Persuade someone to study Latin.
3. Persuade someone to buy a special brand of clothing.
4. Persuade someone to give you a raise at your job.
5. Persuade someone to recycle.

Vocabulary

LATINE	ESPAÑOL	ENGLISH
ecce	¡Mira!	Look!
eheu	¡Ay! ¡Pobre de mi!	Oh dear! Alas!
eugepae	¡Hurra! ¡Qué bien!	Hooray!
minime	¡No! ¡Para nada!	Not at all!
ita vero	¡Sí! ¡Por supuesto!	Yes, indeed!
mirabile	¡Maravilloso! ¡Genial!	Marvelous! Wonderful!
pax	¡Suficiente! ¡Paz! ¡Shhh!	Enough! Peace! Shh!
via	camino, via	road
statua	estatua, imagen	statue, image
caput	cabeza	head

Χαῖρε!

After ξ and o, the next letters of the Greek alphabet are pi (π), rho (ρ), and sigma (σ/ς). Sigmas are unusual: when they appear at the beginning or middle of a word, they look like σ, but when they appear at the end of a word, they look like ς. What letters or combination of letters in our alphabet do you think these letters correspond to? Practice writing pi, rho, and sigma on your own.

$$\Pi\pi \quad P\rho \quad \Sigma\sigma\varsigma$$

LESSON 8.1: Interjections

An **interjection** is a word or a short phrase used to show_______________________________

and is often followed by an _________________________________ .

What are some examples in other languages that you know?

EXERCISE 8.1

Choose an appropriate Latin interjection to match each illustration.

1.________________________

2.________________________

3.________________________

4.________________________

5.________________________

6.________________________

LESSON 8.2: Roman Innovations

The Romans were talented builders and engineers. They created concrete, roads for transportation, aqueducts to carry water, and large buildings and monuments to decorate their city.

Without modern transportation or communication technology (planes, cars, phones, the internet, etc), how did the Romans control such a large empire? The Romans built many roads to keep their large empire connected. The roads extended through modern-day Spain, France, Germany, Africa, and the Middle East. The roads allowed Romans to travel, trade, and send letters through an efficient postal system. Still, news traveled much more slowly than it travels today. For example, it took about 60 days for news from the city of Rome to reach Egypt.

Triumphal arches are one of the most distinctive types of Roman monuments, and a kind of monument that still decorates modern cities today! They were built all over the Roman Empire to celebrate victories in battle. They were normally built across large streets so people could walk through them and admire the architecture and decorations.

Because Roman cities needed so much water, the Romans developed a massive network of aqueducts to bring cold, clean water to the people very quickly, and to flush waste out of the city through Rome's sewage system. The aqueduct channels carry water both above and below ground. Water flows from clean water sources into the cities, pushed by gravity, into the city.

TRIUMPHAL ARCHES: THEN AND NOW

Romans built Triumphal Arches to celebrate emperors, generals, and military victories. This is a practice that we have continued to the present day. The Washington Square Arch in New York City (left) was built in 1892 to celebrate the centennial of George Washington's inauguration as president. The Arc de Triomphe in France (center), completed in 1836, honors those who died in the French Revolution and the Napoleonic Wars. The *Monumento a la Revolución* in Mexico City (right) was completed in 1938 to commemorate the Mexican Revolution.

Χαῖρε!

Eureka! This Greek word is still used today when sudden discoveries are made. It means "I have found it" and was famously exclaimed by the Greek scientist Archimedes when, upon stepping into the bath, he noticed that the water level changed in proportion to his own volume. What exactly did he "find"? Archimedes' "Eureka!" moment can also be called an "Aha!" or a "lightbulb" moment. Have you ever had one of these moments? Can you think of other famous scientists who have?

EXERCISE 8.2

Translate these sentences into English, then identify the interjection in your translation by circling it.

1. Ecce! Mater piscem capit.

____

2. Mirabile! Statua magna est!

____

3. Rex mortuus est. Eheu!

____

4. Ita vero! Semper pugnate ferociter!

____

5. Fatigata sum. Pax!

____

CULTURAL CONNECTION

Due to the Spanish Empire's large influence, Spanish architecture can be seen all around the world today. Spanish architecture was originally inherited from the Romans; when the Romans conquered the area that is now Spain, they brought with them their architectural expertise, building roads, bridges, and aqueducts wherever they went. An example of the Romans' surviving and impressive architecture is the Puente Romano in Mérida, Spain. The Puente Romano is a 790 meter, 2,000 year old bridge-- the oldest and best preserved bridge surviving from Roman times.

Hoy, puedes ver muchos ejemplos de influencia romana en España. Puedes verlo especialmente en el puente romano en Mérida, España. El Puente Romano es 790 metros y tiene 2,000 años; es el puente más viejo y más preservado de los tiempos Romanos.

FIX THE AQUEDUCT!

Help Lucius fix the aqueduct by cutting out the broken pieces and pasting them onto the aqueduct according to which interjection would make the most sense with the story.

In order to get water to the city of Rome, the Romans built aqueducts that carried water from clean sources using the force of gravity. The aqueducts were very useful for the Romans and they were also an impressive sight to behold.

Lucius was a Roman engineer who ensured that the aqueducts worked smoothly. One day he went to work on the aqueduct and water started dripping on his head. He looked around for the source of the dripping water. Eventually he noticed a huge hole in the aqueduct and pointed it out to another engineer!

Lucius wondered what could have caused the aqueduct to break. Suddenly he noticed a Goth behind an archway. He was trying to break the aqueduct and cut off Rome's water supply so that the Goths could invade the city of Rome!

Lucius was not a soldier, but if the aqueducts were broken, the Roman people would not have any clean water. Should he try to fight the Goth and save the city?

Lucius bravely ran towards the Goth and began to fight him! At first Lucius was overpowered. As an engineer, he did not have any weapons or fighting experience. But did that stop Lucius from being brave?

Just as the Goth was about to win the fight, a wolf ran towards them and defended Lucius! The Goth ran away in fear before he could do any more damage. After the Goth was out of sight, Lucius was finally able to get to work fixing the aqueduct!

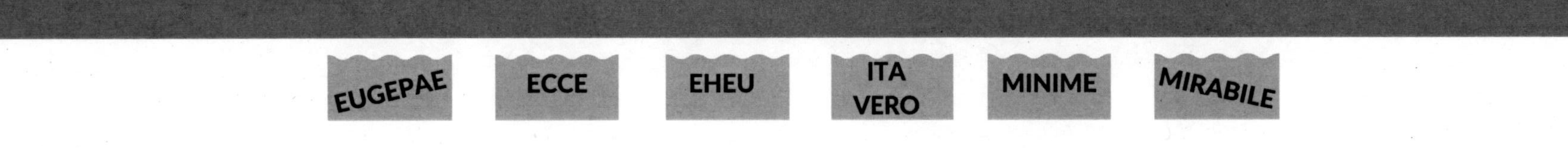

ADDITIONAL NOTES

LESSON 8.3: Perseus and Medusa

There once was a monster named Medusa who lived in a cave at the end of the world. **Ecce Medusa!**

Medusa had the face of a woman, but instead of hair, she had a million snakes sprouting from her head. **Ita vero!** The worst thing about Medusa was not her frightening hair but the fact that whenever anyone looked at Medusa, they turned to stone. **Eheu!**

Hero after hero tried to defeat Medusa, but whenever anyone tried to get close to her, they froze in their tracks, becoming a statue. **Eheu!** Her cave was full of heroes turned to stone. **Ita vero!**

Kings had sent hero after hero to try to defeat Medusa, but without success. **Minime!**

Finally, Perseus was sent on this mission. **Eugepae, Perseus!** Perseus prayed to Minerva and Mercury to help him with this impossible task. Suddenly, they appeared before him with gifts! **Ecce Minerva! Ecce Mercurius!**

They presented him with winged sandals, a magic cap that made him invisible, a sharp sword, a sack, and a shield that was so polished that you could use it as a mirror. **Mirabile!** Perseus used the winged sandals and the cap to fly to the end of the world without any trouble. **Ita vero!**

He made it to Medusa's cave, and as he entered, he held the shield up in front of his face so that he would be able to fight Medusa by looking at the reflection in his shield instead of seeing her face. Then he would not turn to stone. **Mirabile!**

Perseus drew his sword and cut off her terrible head. While still looking away he put it into his sack. **Eugepae!**

Perseus flew home with the head of Medusa in his sack. **Eugepae!**

Now Perseus had the best weapon he could possibly want to defeat his enemies! **Mirabile!**

To thank Minerva for her help, he gave the head of Medusa to her, and she put it on her shield. **Ita vero! Eugepae! Mirabile!**

DISCUSSION QUESTIONS

According to every myth that we know, Medusa never left her cave—so the only people that she turned to stone were these so-called heroes that invaded her home trying to kill her. Write a short story from Medusa's perspective.

Often in mythology and stories, heroes are sent on a quest, but they are given magical items to help them along the way. Can you think of other examples of a character from a book or movie who went on a journey with powerful tools to help?

Earlier we learned about the hero, Theseus, and his defeat of the minotaur. How is the myth of Perseus similar to Theseus? How are they different?

Just as the shield of Perseus shows reflections, sometimes myths can reflect real historical events—but in an exaggerated way. Some scholars who study myths and cultures suspect that Medusa was originally a goddess that was worshipped by a matriarchal society. Then a patriarchal society took over. They saw images and statues of the goddess Medusa, but they viewed her differently. How does this myth reflect this possible history?

EXERCISE 8.3

Match each English derivative with its Latin root by writing the Latin root and its meaning in the chart below. All the words are from Unit 8 vocabulary. Then, underline, circle, or highlight the letters that the roots have in common with their English derivative. The first one has been completed for you.

ENGLISH DERIVATIVES	LATIN ROOT
verify= to make sure something is true	ita **ver**o=yes, indeed!
pacifist	
admire	
decapitate	

In the following sentences, the underlined words are English derivatives. Using your knowledge of their Latin derivatives, what do you think these words mean?

1. Before they let him into the office, they made sure to **verify** his documents.

   a) To shred   b) To prosecute   c) To arrange   d) To check that it is true

2. The **pacifist** refused to join the army despite the pressure from the government.

   a) Person who prefers peace   b) Person with large hands   c) Farmer   d) Cheese lover

3. The boy **admired** the soccer players on the field.

   a) Threw peanuts at them   b) Made fun of   c) Took pictures of   d) Regard with respect

4. Perseus **decapitated** Medusa with his sword.

   a) Cut off her head   b) Stabbed   c) Saw the reflection of   d) Knighted

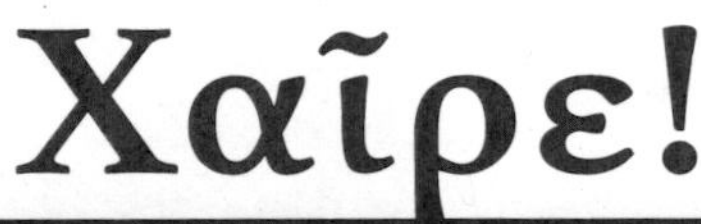

Χαῖρε!

After Perseus cut off Medusa's head, Pegasus, the flying horse, and Chrysaor were born. They sprang from Medusa's neck! Where might you have seen a depiction of a pegasus?

Vocabulary

LATINE	ESPAÑOL	ENGLISH
et	Y	and
-que	Y (colocada al final de una palabra)	and (attached to the end of a word)
sed	pero	but
aut	O	or
quamquam	aunque, a pesar de	although
quod	porque	because
deus/a	dios/diosa	god/goddess
templum	templo	temple
festum	festividad	holiday
arbor	árbol	tree

Χαῖρε!

After π, ρ, and σ/ς, the next letters of the Greek alphabet are tau (τ) and upsilon (υ). What letters or combination of letters in our alphabet do you think these letters correspond to? Practice writing tau and upsilon on your own.

Ττ Υυ

LESSON 9.1: Conjunctions

A **conjunction** is a word that joins or connects _______________________, _______________________,

or _______________________.

For example:

Joining words : I like apples **and** oranges.

Joining phrases : Yesterday I went home, ate a snack, **and** practiced playing the tambourine.

Joining clauses : I ate the apple, **although** I found a worm inside.

EXERCISE 9.1

Translate the following sentences into English. In your translation, identify the conjunctions by circling them.

1. Quamquam Iuppiter est magnus deus, amo Saturnum.

----

2. Miles fugit sed non vincit iterum.

----

3. Ego edo caseum panemque.

----

4. Tu es miser quod tu es fatigatus.

----

5. Quid tibi nomen est et quid agis?

----

6. Ego specto templa et arbores.

LESSON 9.2: Roman Religion

Read the text about Roman religion below. The text contains Latin words in bold.

The Romans believed in many **di** (gods) and **deae** and they believed these deities controlled different parts of nature and human society like the ocean, war, marriage, farming, crafts, and many other things.

For example, **Pluto** was the god of the underworld. You read a little about him in Lesson 3.3. The underworld is the world of the dead, just below the land of the living. It is common for mythological heroes to journey to the underworld, like in Disney's *Hercules*.

In Greek mythology, it is called **Hades** and is guarded by the three-headed dog, **Cerberus**. To enter the underworld, one must cross the **River Styx**. When a person died, his/her relatives would place a coin on the person's lips to pay the ferryman, **Charon**, and ensure entry.

The Romans believed that one's soul was immortal, so when a person died his/her soul would be judged by **Pluto**. If a person had done good while living, he/she was sent to **Elysium**. If a person did not do good while living, he/she was sent to **Tartarus**. These places are similar to what some modern-day religions refer to as heaven and hell.

The Romans built huge, beautiful **templa** for their **di** and **deae** throughout their empire. Inside these **templa** were **statuae** of the **di** for whom the **templa** were built. The Romans believed that the **di** and **deae** would help them if they gave them sacrifices, so they made offerings like meat, incense, spices, flowers, and money at the **templa**.

The Romans also honored their **di** and **deae** with **festa**. All of the major gods had a festival day. These **festa** were paid for by wealthy Romans or by the government, and the Roman people could attend them for free.

They also worshiped **di** and **deae** at home. They believed in household spirits who protected the **familia**. Members of the **familia** made offerings of food and drink to shrines in their homes and prayed for good luck and safety.

Χαῖρε!

Have you ever heard of the Pope? The Pope is the head of the Roman Catholic church and lives in Vatican City. One of his many titles is *pontifex maximus*. This comes from the title given to the chief priest in the ancient city of Rome.

To become a priest, one must first go to school to learn theology. The word theology is derived from the Greek words θεός (god) and λόγος (word/study), meaning "the study of god" or "the study of the gods."

EXERCISE 9.2

Match each English derivative with its Latin root by writing the Latin root and its meaning in the chart below. All the words are from Unit 9 vocabulary. Then underline, circle, or highlight the letters that the roots have in common with their English derivative. The first one has been completed for you.

ENGLISH DERIVATIVES	LATIN ROOT
deities	deus/dea=god/goddess
arboretum	
festive	
templar	

In the following sentences, the underlined words are English derivatives. Using your knowledge of their Latin roots, what do you think these words mean?

1. In museums today you can see many statues of Roman **deities**.

    a) Buildings   b) Gods   c) Soldiers   d) Rulers

2. Do you want to visit the **arboretum** with me?

    a) Temple   b) Place to buy things   c) Zoo   d) Park for trees

3. The house was decorated to look **festive**.

    a) Sad   b) Expensive   c) Celebratory   d) Minimal

4. He was a member of the Knights **Templar**.

    a) A religious group of knights   b) Exiled knights   c) The king's guard
    d) Well-educated knights

ZOOM IN

Perhaps you've seen a symbol of a snake wrapped around a rod on the side of ambulances or at your doctor's office. This is the Rod of Asclepius. Asclepius was the ancient god of medicine and healing. His rod has become the dominant symbol for healthcare. But this symbol of healing is often confused with the caduceus of Mercury, a staff with two snakes and wings that Mercury used to lead souls to the underworld. How are these two symbols similar? What is the irony in getting these symbols mixed up?

LESSON 9.3: Baucis and Philemon

Once upon a time the **deus** Jupiter **et** the deus Mercury came down from Mount Olympus **et** disguised themselves as mortals. **Quamquam** they were **di**, they both transformed themselves into old men with walking sticks **et** travelled to a town of mortals. In the town they went from **domus** to **domus** in search of food **et** shelter, **sed** no matter whether the **domus** was **magnus et** richly decorated, **aut** more modest, they were turned away at each door **quod** the villagers were unwilling to welcome strangers.

Finally, they came to the simple rustic **casa** of an elderly couple named Baucis **et** Philemon. It was certainly the smallest **et** simplest **casa** they had seen in the town, **sed** neither Baucis nor Philemon hesitated to welcome the disguised **di** inside. **Quamquam** they had little, their generosity far surpassed their neighbors. Instead of turning

the **di** away, they apologized that they could only offer the little food **et vinum** they had. **Quamquam** they had so little, they laid out the table with simple **panis et caseus** and carefully divided their small portion of **vinum** in the guests' cups. They expected the **vinum** to **celeriter** disappear, **sed** suddenly it seemed to refill itself in the jug. Baucis looked at Philemon in surprise, and they asked themselves **cur** this was happening. Then, Jupiter **et** Mercury revealed that they were **di**!

Both the old man **et** woman got off their chairs to kneel before the **di** in supplication **et** prayer. Philemon then ran outside **et capit** their only goose so that they could serve their glorious guests, **sed** the goose broke free **et** ran straight to the safety of Jupiter's lap. He caught it **et** reassured the couple that they need not slay their only goose, **sed** that they should leave the town **et** climb the hill.

When they returned, their humble cottage had been transformed into an ornate **templum**. Baucis **et** Philemon returned to their home **et** became guardians of the **templum,** continuing to welcome any guests who came to offer prayers. They asked only one favor of Jupiter and Mercury, that when one of them should pass away, the other would die at the same time. The couple's wish was granted **et** when they died, Jupiter transformed the pair into entwined **arbores** in the courtyard of the **templum**.

DISCUSSION QUESTIONS

Why did Mercury and Jupiter come down to visit the mortals?

How did Baucis and Philemon realize they were in the presence of the gods?

Why were Baucis and Philemon rewarded by the gods?

What did Baucis and Philemon request from the gods? How did the gods fulfill their request?

What does this myth teach Romans about how to treat strangers?

EXERCISE 9.3

After reading the story of Baucis and Philemon, which Latin conjunction fits best in the blanks? After you have filled in the blanks, number the sentences in the order that they happened in the story.

☐ _________________ Baucis and Philemon filled the cups of the guests, the wine never ran out!

☐ Jupiter granted the couple's wish, ___________________________ they had been kind to strangers.

☐ Whether the house was large ______________ small, they all turned away the gods in disguise.

☐ The couple tried to sacrifice their pet goose to the gods, ________ Jupiter would not let them.

☐ Jupiter ______________ Mercury decided to visit mortals in disguise.

Χαῖρε!

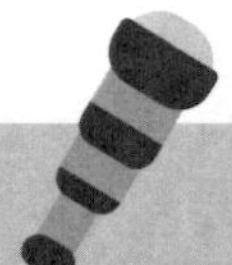

ZOOM IN

The tire company Goodyear's logo features a boot with wings. This was the symbol of Mercury, the god of travelers. He was able to travel quickly using his winged boots. Why woulds a tire company want to associate itself with Mercury?

ADDITIONAL NOTES

ADDITIONAL NOTES

Vocabulary

LATINE	ESPAÑOL	ENGLISH
in	en	in, at
ad	a, hacia	to, toward
ab	de	away from
trans	al otro lado de	across
ex	fuera de	out of
inter	entre	between
per	através	through
super	encima de	above, over
sub	debajo de	under
circum	alrededor de/cerca	around

LESSON 10.1: Prepositions

A **preposition** is a word that tells you where a noun is, or its _______________________ in relation to another noun, showing

_______________________ (above, under, near),

_______________________ (before, after, during), or

_______________________ (towards, out of).

Can you think of other prepositions in English?

What part of the word "preposition" gives you a hint as to what it means?

A preposition is often used with a noun in a **prepositional** _______________.

Example: "over the hill," "through the woods," "to the house"

In the following sentences, underline the whole prepositional phrase, then circle the preposition.

The monkey on the tree branch is giggling.

After the battle, the soldiers were tired.

I want to go to the library.

CULTURAL CONNECTION

In the year 70 CE, the Romans founded the colony Emerita Augusta, known today as Mérida. This city was the capital of Lusitania, a Roman province located in the region of Hispania. Lusitania occupied a large part of modern Portugal, and a small part of Spain. Emerita Augusta was founded by Emperor Augustus with the purpose of giving retired soldiers a place to settle after serving in the army. The other inhabitants of the city were Lusitanians (the original settlers of the region) who had become citizens of Rome. The Latin word *emeritus* means retired or veteran.

Uno de las ciudades romanas en Hispania es la ciudad de Emerita Angustia, que ahora se llama Mérida. El imperator Augustus creó esta ciudad para dar un hogar a los veteranos de guerra.

EXERCISE 10.1

Translate the following sentences into English. In your translation, underline the prepositional phrase and circle the preposition.

1. Ego specto lupum sub arbore.

---

2. Quis pugnat circum domum?

---

3. Tu ambulas* ad aquam.   (*ambulare = to walk)

---

4. Eheu! Ecce! Gladius est super caput tibi!

---

5. Puella ambulat trans templum.

---

6. Discipuli ambulant ex ianua.

---

7. Cur magister fugit per fenestram?

---

8. Nos fugimus lente ab via.

---

9. Valida mater et bellus pater edunt in villa.

Χαῖρε!

After τ and υ, the next letters of the Greek alphabet are phi (φ) chi (χ), and psi (ψ). What letters or combination of letters in our alphabet do you think these letters correspond to? Practice writing phi, chi, and psi on your own.

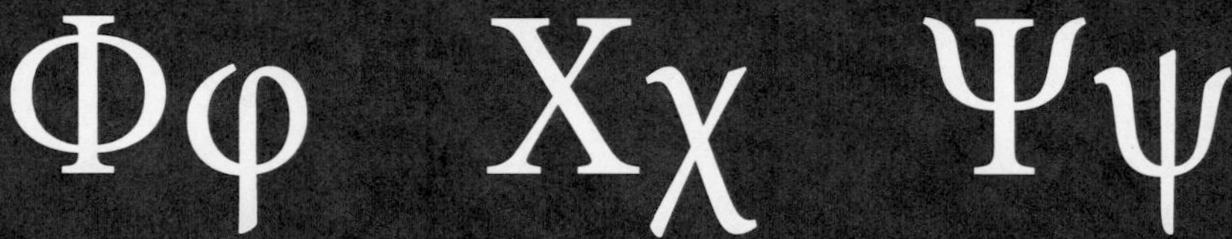

LESSON 10.2: The City of Rome

The city of Rome is located in central Italy on the Tiber River. It was built on seven hills. Today, Rome is the capital of Italy. If you visit modern-day Rome, you can still see ruins of the ancient buildings and imagine the lives of men, women, and children who lived there long ago.

Wealthy Romans lived in large houses called **domus**, but most Romans lived in small apartment buildings called **insulae**. The **insulae** could be quite cramped, but Romans spent much time in public spaces in the city – conducting business in the **Forum**, socializing in public baths, or public games, like gladiatorial fights and chariot races.

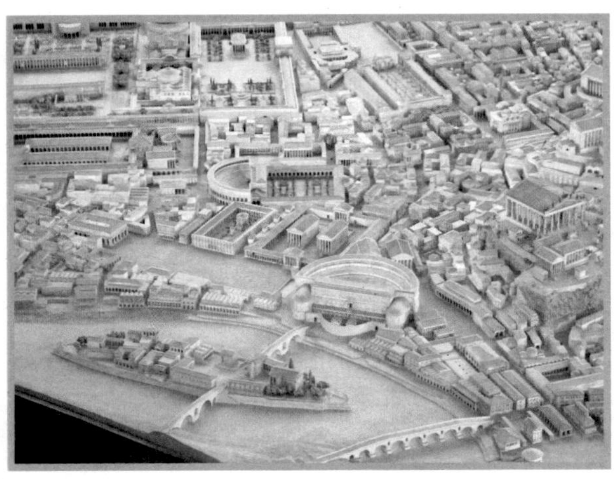

The Forum was the busy center of public life in ancient Rome. The Forum was filled with public buildings, markets, monuments, and religious temples. Legal trials, speeches, and political elections took place here.

The **Colosseum** was an ancient amphitheater where Romans would watch gladiatorial games. The **Circus Maximus** was a large stadium where Romans would come to watch chariot races. Today, the Circus Maximus is a public park and is still occasionally used for concerts and events. You could say it has been entertaining the masses for centuries!

Most Romans bathed and exercised in large public bathing complexes; bathing was an important part of Roman social life as well as Roman hygiene.

EXERCISE 10.2

Look at the following Latin verbs. These are called compound verbs because they have a Latin root with a preposition attached to them. You already know the Latin roots and the prepositions separately. Now see if you can match each word with its correct translation on the right.

_______ 1. absum

_______ 2. inspecto

_______ 3. adsum

_______ 4. abdico

_______ 5. intersum

_______ 6. avoco (ab + voco)

_______ 7. intercipio

_______ 8. advenio

_______ 9. perficio

_______ 10. invenio

A. I am here

B. I arrive

C. I finish

D. I look inside

E. I am away

F. I find, I come upon

G. I deny, renounce

H. I distract

I. I am between

J. I interrupt

> **WORDS TO HELP**
>
> sum = I am
> dico = I say, I speak
> voco = I call
> venio = I come
> facio = I make, I do

Χαῖρε!

The Greek word for fire was πῦρ (*pur,* or *pyr*). Today, it forms the root "pyro-" which can be found in many English words relating to fire. What words have you heard which begin with "pyro-"?

LESSON 10.3: Aeneas' Voyage

The ancient Romans told many stories about their origins. Though they believed that Romulus founded the city of Rome, they traced the beginning of Roman civilization in Italy back even earlier than Romulus to a hero named Aeneas. Aeneas was the son of the goddess Venus and he lived in Troy, a city in modern-day Turkey.

Aeneas est filius deae Veneris. Aeneas est heros Troianus.

WORDS TO HELP

Veneris—of Venus
Graeci—Greeks
navigat—sails
regina—queen
sola—alone
adiuvat—helps
venit—comes

According to legend, Aeneas fought in the Trojan War, a war between Troy and Greece. The war lasted 10 years until, finally, the Greeks won and destroyed Troy. Aeneas and his family were in the city as the Greeks burned it to the ground. The gods knew that Aeneas had a great destiny and they told him to flee from Troy and establish a new kingdom. Aeneas took his small son Ascanius and his old father and ran to the ships with the other fleeing Trojans.

Troiani et Graeci pugnant. Graeci vincunt. Aeneas et filius Ascanius et pater fugiunt.

The Trojans set sail with Aeneas to look for a new homeland. First, they sailed to North Africa where they met Dido, the powerful Queen of Carthage. Dido and her people had also been suddenly displaced, but she was a strong, clever leader and helped them found a new and growing kingdom. When Aeneas saw Dido, he admired so much about her and quickly fell in love. She fell in love with Aeneas too, but Aeneas was destined to found his own kingdom

and could not stay in Carthage. Once again, the gods told Aeneas he must leave to seek the Trojans' new homeland. He left Dido broken-hearted and furious over his unfulfilled promises to her. She cursed him and his descendants as his ships sailed away—and some say this was the start of the hostility between the future Romans and Carthaginians many centuries later.

Aeneas navigat ad Carthaginem. Aeneas et regina Dido amant. Aeneas navigat iterum. Dido sola et misera et irata est.

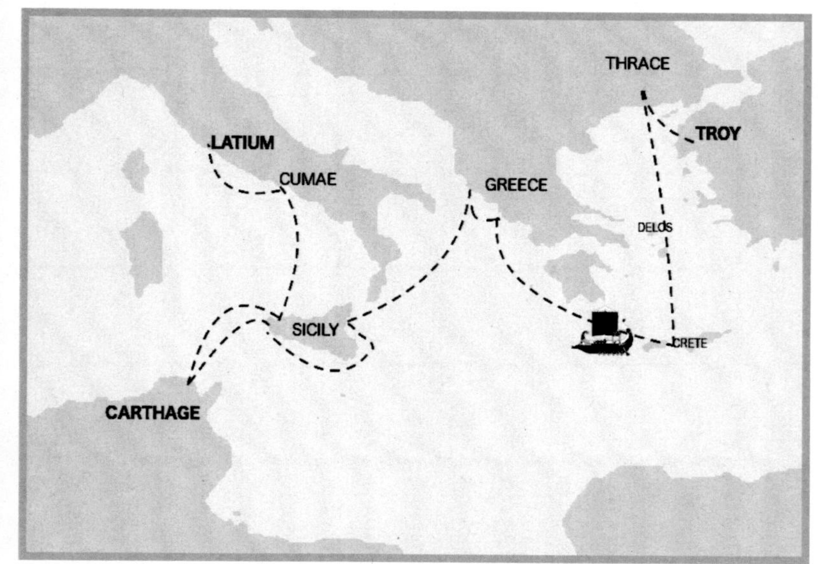

Aeneas traveled far and wide with no idea where to find this destined land. He was so lost that he decided to ask the Sibyl, a famous prophetess who knew all things. She advised him that he needed to first visit the underworld, the land of the dead, and from there he would know the way to his new homeland.

Aeneas navigat diu. Sybil adiuvat Aenean.

Aeneas traveled down to the underworld and saw many strange and frightening things. He met old friends and warriors who had died at Troy, but he also discovered that he was destined to found his new kingdom in Italy. He took his ships and people to Italy and found that another group of people already lived there. These people called themselves Latins and lived peacefully in the land they called Latium.

The Latin king welcomed Aeneas and his Trojan people to Latium. When Aeneas met the King's daughter, Lavinia, he knew that she was meant to be his wife and that this would be the new homeland for the Trojan people. Aeneas was the ancestor of Romulus and Remus.

Aeneas venit ad Italiam. Latium in Italia est.

DISCUSSION QUESTIONS

How do you imagine Aeneas felt during his long journey?

Do you think it was fair that Aeneas founded a new kingdom on the Latins' land? Why or why not?

If one of the most important Roman heroes came from far away and settled on Italian land, what does this say about what the Romans thought it meant to be "Roman"?

The Romans had multiple foundation myths. Choose a place you know well—it could be a country, or a city, or even your neighborhood—if you had to tell a story about its foundation, where would you start?

EXERCISE 10.3

Match each English derivative with its Latin root by writing the Latin root and its meaning in the chart below. All the words are from Unit 10 vocabulary. Then, underline, circle, or highlight the letters that the roots have in common with their English derivative. The first one has been completed for you.

ENGLISH DERIVATIVES	LATIN ROOT
superior	**super**=above, upper
interact	
exterior	
suboptimal	

In the following sentences, the bold words are English derivatives. Using your knowledge of their Latin roots, what do you think these words mean?

1. The Romans overthrew their kings so that one person would not be **superior** to the other citizens.

   a) Friendlier   b) Higher-ranking   c) Meaner   d) The best farmer

2. My friend does not **interact** with people much because he is shy.

   a) To communicate or be involved with someone   b) To scream   c) To whisper
   d) To tell scary stories

3. The **exterior** of the building is covered in graffiti.

   a) Ground   b) Outer surface   c) Roof   d) Stairs

4. The windy weather was **suboptimal** for a beach day.

   a) Perfect   b) Attracting sharks   c) Unfamiliar   d) Less than great

UBI EST AENEAS?

Can you help Aeneas find his way? Cut out all of the white spaces below. Cut out and insert the pull tab from the materials. As you guide Aeneas along his journey, write Latin sentences in the space near "Ubi est Aeneas?" to describe his location.

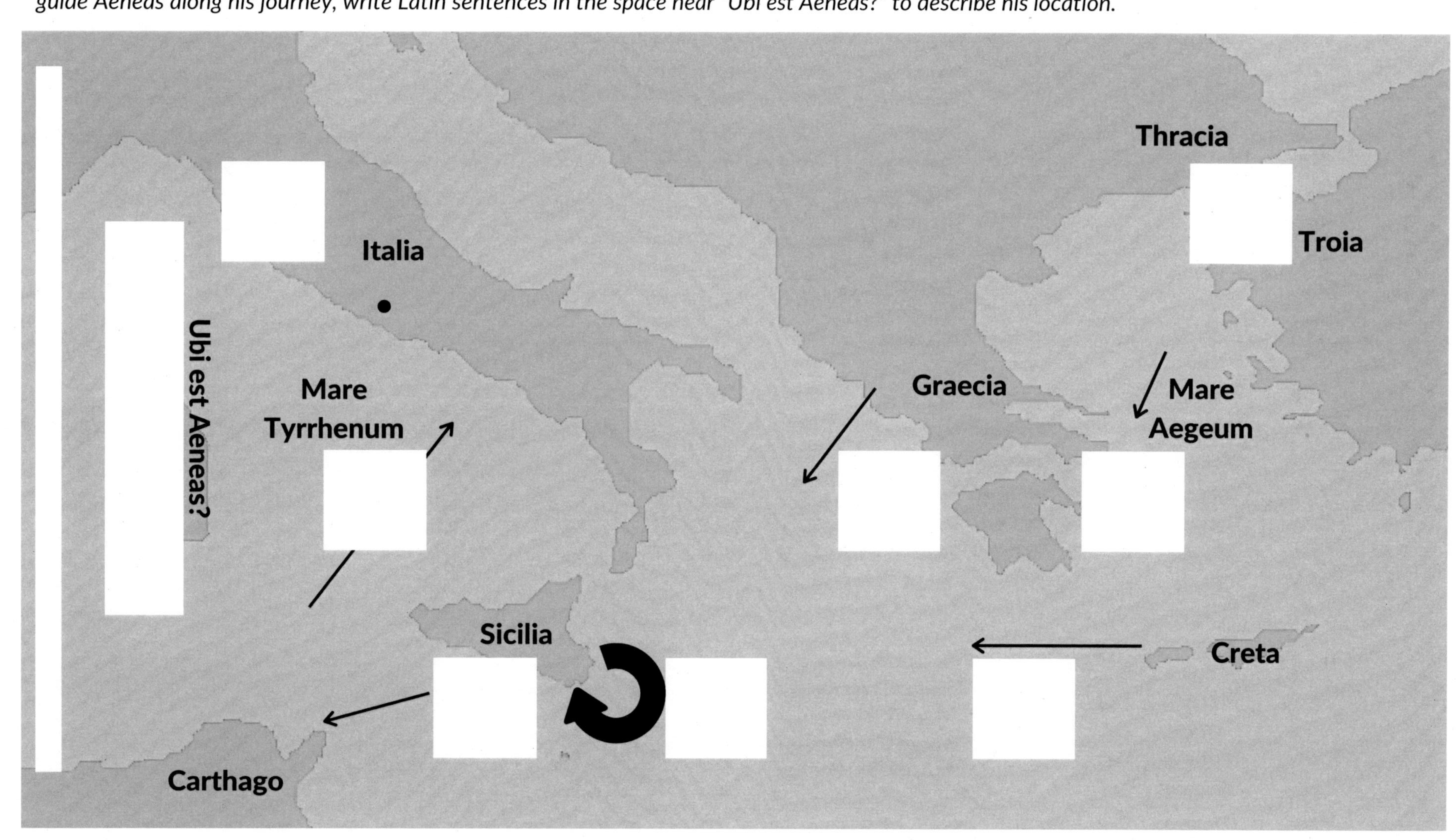

ADDITIONAL NOTES

Vocabulary

ROMAN NUMERAL	LATIN WORD	SPANISH	ENGLISH
I	unus, una, unum	uno	one
II	duo	dos	two
III	tres	tres	three
IV	quattuor	cuatro	four
V	quinque	cinco	five
VI	sex	seis	six
VII	septem	siete	seven
VIII	octo	ocho	eight
IX	novem	nueve	nine
X	decem	diez	ten
C	centum	cien	one hundred
M	mille	mil	one thousand

LESSON 11.1: Roman Numerals

Today, we have symbols for numbers like 1, 2, 3, as well as words for numbers like one, two, three. The Romans also had symbols for their numbers, and we call these Roman numerals. These are the basic numerals Romans used:

I = 1   X = 10   C = 100

V = 5   L = 50   M = 1000

For numbers in between these, put the symbol to the **right** of the number to add onto it. For example:

III = I (1) + I + I = 3   VII = V (5) + I (1) + I (1) = 7   LXV = L (50) + X (10) + V (5) = 65

You won't ever have four or more in a row of the same symbol, except for M because it is the biggest. If you place a numeral with a smaller value **to the left** of a numeral with a larger value, it **subtracts** from that numeral.

For 4, instead of IIII, you'd write IV, because V(5) - I(1) = 4

For 9, instead of VIIII, you'd write IX because X(10) - I(1) = 9

And you can do a combination of adding and subtracting, for example:

CMLV = (M - C) + (L + V) = 955

WHAT ABOUT CMLIV?

ZOOM IN

Roman numerals are used in modern advertisements, notably for the Super Bowl! The NFL numbers each championship game using Roman numerals instead of standard numbers. Which Super Bowl's logo is this? Why do you think they use Roman numerals instead of regular numbers?

Χαῖρε!

You've made it! After φ, χ, and ψ, the very last letter of the Greek alphabet is omega (ω). What letters or combination of letters in our alphabet do you think this letter corresponds to? Practice writing omega on your own.

ROMAN NUMERALS

Some numbers have been left blank. What do you think the numbers or numerals should be where there are blanks?

I = 1	XI = 11	XXV = ☐	CV = ☐
II = 2	XII = 12	XXIX = 29	☐ = 150
III = 3	XIII = 13	XX = 30	CCC = ☐
IV = 4	XIV = 14	XL = 40	☐ = 400
V = 5	XV = 15	XLV = ☐	D = 500
VI = 6	☐ = 16	L = 50	DC = ☐
VII = 7	XVII = 17	LX = ☐	CM = ☐
VIII = 8	XVIII = ☐	☐ = 75	M = 1000
IX = 9	XIX = 19	☐ = 90	MM = ☐
X = 10	XX = 20	C = 100	MMD = ☐

Let's practice converting the following to Roman numerals:

What day of the month is it?

If the Roman Empire fell in CDLXXVI , what year is that?

Make up a number and then convert it to Roman numerals!

What is your birthday in Roman Numerals?
Month: **Day:**   **Year:**

Χαῖρε!

There were many famous ancient Greek mathematicians, several of whom had large followings in their own time. Have you ever heard of Pythagoras? He is now famous for discovering the Pythagorean theorem, which explains the relation between the sides of a right triangle. To the ancient Greeks and Romans, he was just as well-known for teaching vegetarianism based on his belief in reincarnation.

EXERCISE 11.1

Answer the following simple math problems in Roman Numerals and Latin words when you can.

#	Problem	Roman Numerals	Latin number word
1	Unum + tria =		
2	Octo + duo =		
3	Decem—quattuor =		
4	Centum x decem =		
5	Novem—duo =		
6	XXV + XL =		
7	DV + LXII =		
8	MM—M =		
9	CD + CCXL =		
10	XXV + IV =		

ZOOM IN

You may have seen Roman numerals used in various places all around you—such as clocks and monuments. Can you convert the numerals on this replica of the Liberty Bell? Why do you think we choose to put Roman numerals on these places instead of using regular Arabic numbers? Try to find as many Roman numerals as you can today—who can spot them first?

LESSON 11.2: Roman Coins

We can learn a lot about the ancient Romans through reading Latin literature, but this only tells us part of the story— oftentimes the story of the most elite Romans who had time to study and learn to read and write literature. Another way to learn about the ancient Romans is to study the ruins of buildings that the Romans left behind, and studying objects from the ancient world, like coins. Archaeologists excavate, or dig up, cities and towns and study ancient objects to learn more about Roman culture.

Roman coins were made of bronze, silver, and gold, and came in different sizes, similar to our quarters, nickels, and dimes.

E PLURIBUS UNUM

Now that you know Latin, you'll find short Latin phrases on monuments and buildings in the US. You'll also find Latin on our currency. The back of the quarter and penny contains the phrase *e pluribus unum*. If *e* is another way of writing the Latin preposition *ex* and *pluribus* is a Latin word that means "many", what does the phrase mean? Why is this a meaningful phrase in the United States?

There were images on both sides of Roman coins, much like our coins today. The earliest Roman coins depicted heads of gods and goddesses like Venus, Mars, and Jupiter. Later on, most coins displayed the heads of emperors on one side and monuments on the other. Coins were one way that emperors and other elite Romans displayed their power.

Studying Roman coins can tell us a lot about the Roman Empire. When we dig up a Roman coin somewhere in the world, we know that the Romans traded in that place. The images on the coin (which emperor is depicted, for example) can help us figure out when the Romans were trading in that place.

EXERCISE 11.2

Translate the following sentences into English.

1. Nos edimus septem pisces quod nos amamus pisces.

____

2. Fratres capiunt quinque gladios ex casa.

____

3. Vos estis tres magni milites et vos pugnatis ferociter.

____

4. Ego non timeo unum iratum imperatorem.

____

5. Tu fugis ab novem lupis in forum.

____

CULTURAL CONNECTION

In Spanish, the word for coin, *moneda*, comes from the Latin word for money, *moneta*. The drawing of the coin below is a reproduction of a coin that was found in Merida, Spain. The side of the coin shown in the drawing depicts the gates of the city, and it bears the inscription *Augusta Emerita*. Using what you learned in the previous lesson, if you had 10 coins from Augusta Emerita, how would you express that in Spanish? How would you write it in Roman numerals?

QUANTUM PECUNIAE

Quintus has many errands to complete at the Square of Corporations in Ostia. Paste your money pouch from materials at the start, creating a pocket to hold your XXX coins. Roll the dice at each location to see how much pecuniae Quintus spends there. Calculate how much money he has left each time he makes a purchase. At the end, how much money will he have left?

Paste here

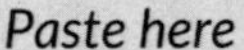

Paste here

Location III
How much pecuniae did
Quintus spend?
(Scribe Latine)

How much pecuniae does
Quintus have left?
(Scribe Roman Numerals)

Paste here

Location I
How much pecuniae did
Quintus spend?
(Scribe Latine)

How much pecuniae does
Quintus have left?
(Scribe Roman Numerals)

Location IV
How much pecuniae did
Quintus spend?
(Scribe Latine)

How much pecuniae does
Quintus have left?
(Scribe Roman Numerals)

Paste here

Location II
How much pecuniae did
Quintus spend?
(Scribe Latine)

How much pecuniae does
Quintus have left?
(Scribe Roman Numerals)

Location V
How much pecuniae did
Quintus spend?
(Scribe Latine)

How much pecuniae does
Quintus have left?
(Scribe Roman Numerals)

Paste here

Quantum does Quintus have left?

(Scribe Latine)

(Scribe Roman Numerals)

What can Quintus buy next?

I-II: panem	X-XIV: librum
III-IV: caseum	XV-XX: avem
V-VI: tabulam	XXI-XXIV: canem
VII-IX: parvam statuam	

ADDITIONAL NOTES

LESSON 11.3: Hercules and the Hydra

Once there was a terrible monster called the Hydra. The Hydra was a gigantic water-serpent who lived in a swampy lake and would rise up from the murky waters to terrorize the countryside. It had nine terrible heads which would spit poisonous venom on its victims.

One day the Hydra ate one hundred villagers.

Responde Latine: **Quot townspeople did the Hydra** *edit*?

Responde Latine: **Quot capita did the Hydra have?**

The hero, Hercules, was tasked with saving the people from this awful monster. Hercules had heard that the Hydra not only had nine heads but that when one of the heads was cut off two would grow back in its place. One of these heads was even immortal and could never be killed!

Responde Latine: **Quot immortal** *capita* **did the Hydra have?**

Responde Latine: **Quot capita would grow back when one was severed?**

Hercules was not daunted by this frightening monster. He decided to bring his nephew, Iolus, with him to help him fight the Hydra. He knew that the Hydra would try to lure them into the swampy waters and drown them there, so he shot seven fire-tipped arrows into the Hydra's lair to force the monster out. As it emerged from the cave, Hercules seized it and started attacking its many heads.

Responde Latine: **Quot people did it take** *pugnare* **the Hydra?**

Responde Latine: **Quot fire-tipped arrows did he shoot** *ad* **the Hydra?**

As soon as he cut off one head, two more would burst forth in its place, so Hercules called for Iolus to help. Iolus held a torch to the Hydra's neck after Hercules cut off its head and thus prevented more heads from sprouting on the monster. Together they cut off all eight of the Hydra's mortal heads and then Hercules sliced the immortal head off of the Hydra and packed it away into a sack. Then he dipped a thousand of his arrows into the Hydra's poisonous blood. He buried this head deep in the ground and in order to be extra certain that the Hydra would never haunt the villagers again. He rolled a giant boulder on top of the buried head.

Responde Latine: **Quot** arrows did Hercules dip in the Hydra's blood?

Responde Latine: **Quot** mortal *capita* did Hercules cut off?

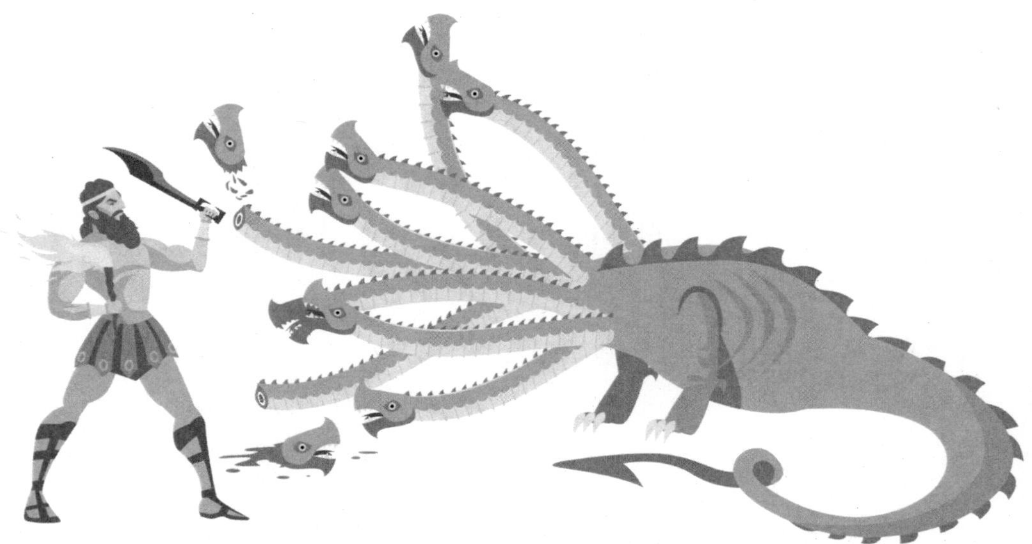

DISCUSSION QUESTIONS

Like Hercules facing the Hydra, sometimes when we try to solve a problem, we end up causing more problems. Has this ever happened to you? Discuss a time in your life when you faced such a problem and how you dealt with it.

Mythology inspires scientists too! The Hydra is a real creature named after the mythological monster. Research the real hydra and discuss the similarities it has with the fictional Hydra.

Killing the Hydra was one of twelve labors that Hercules had to complete to prove he was a hero. However, after defeating the monster, he was told that this labor would not count because he had the help of Iolus. He went on to perform another heroic task! Have you ever worked really hard at something and found out your work was unappreciated? How did this make you feel? What lessons can you learn from how Hercules handled this news?

EXERCISE 11.3

Match each English derivative with its Latin root by writing the Latin root and its meaning in the chart below. All the words are from Unit 11 vocabulary. Then, underline, circle, or highlight the letters that the roots have in common with their English derivative. The first one has been completed for you.

ENGLISH DERIVATIVES	LATIN ROOT
Unity	**Un**us, **un**a, **un**um—one
Century	
Sextuplet	
Dual	

In the following sentences, the underlined words are English derivatives. Using your knowledge of their Latin roots, what do you think these words mean?

1. The Roman Empire lacked **unity**, so it split in half and eventually completely fell apart
   a) Candy b) Soldiers c) Ability to fly d) Being joined as one whole

2. My grandmother was born in 1915, so she has lived over a **century**.
   a) Period of one hundred years b) period with lots of wars c) Variety of leaders
   d) Period of ten years

3. She gave birth to **sextuplets**—four boys and two girls.
   a) Dogs b) Six children at birth c) Seven children at birth d) Aliens

4. My best friend was born in Italy, but she was raised in Canada, so she now has **dual** citizenship.
   a) Consisting of two parts b) Zero c) honorary d) Consisting of eight parts

ZOOM IN

In 1997, Disney produced the movie *Hercules*, which featured the mythological son of Zeus as the main character. In the film, he uses his great strength to help his father and the other gods battle the Titans who are led by Hades. They are trying to overthrow Mount Olympus, the home of the gods. Why do you think Disney made this allusion to classical mythology? How did they change the myth from the original myth? Why do you think they made these changes?

WORD	DEFINITION
drama	writing meant for performance in a theater
comedy	a humorous play about amusing characters overcoming challenges
tragedy	a sad play about the downfall of an important character
satyr plays	plays that used physical humor to mock familiar characters
pantomime	drama without words, performed with gestures, dance, or other spectacle
chorus	a group of performers that were part of Greek dramas, narrating, commenting, and interacting with the main characters in different ways

The Greeks are often given credit for inventing the first dramatic plays. Originally, a group of actors known as the **chorus** would recite poems and songs about history or mythology, along with dancing on stage. One day, an actor from the chorus delivered his own lines and interacted with the chorus—creating the first dialogue and a new form of dramatic art. The Greeks had three main types of plays—**comedy, tragedy,** and **satyr plays**.

A Greek **tragedy** was about a noble character who goes through terrible circumstances and sorrows—often of his or her own making. A **comedy** might be about more common characters and their adventures, while a **satyr play** was usually more physical humor that mocked various characters from mythology or current news.

All Greek plays featured song and dance and invited the audience to consider lofty ideals of philosophy, history, or current political events.

The Romans always had a hunger for entertainment, and their earliest forms were adopted from the Etruscans. Early Roman theater featured songs, dances, and acrobatic feats. As their territory grew and they encountered new cultures, they were inspired by Greek forms of theater and the Roman stage showed plays that were translations or loose adaptations of Greek plays. The Romans didn't copy the idea of the **chorus** in their plays, but they did add music to go along with the words. For the Greeks, violent actions were reported by a messenger and weren't portrayed on stage, but the Romans loved gore and would reenact violent scenes of combat or death for their bloodthirsty crowds. Soon they developed their own popular playwrights, like Plautus and Terence, though the themes and characters still echoed a Greek influence. Romans were not as interested in philosophy as the Greeks, so they soon favored performances without words called **pantomime**, where the story was told through dramatic gestures, costumes, and spectacle.

In both Greek and Roman theater, the actors wore masks to help emphasize the facial features of their characters from far away. Feminine masks were especially useful because men played women's parts, and female actors weren't allowed until much later. The mouth of the mask was also shaped in such a way to help project their voices—like a megaphone! For both groups, plays were performed for special occasions. The Greeks held theater contests and throughout the competition, they honored Dionysus, the god of theatre, fertility, and merry-making. The Romans would hold performances for many different festivals and events throughout the year—it could be for a public holiday honoring any of the gods, or a political official might pay for a day of entertainment in order to win favor from the Roman people.

Χαῖρε!

The word "tragedy" comes from the Greek word, τραγῳδία, meaning "goat-song," but no one is quite sure why. Perhaps a goat was sacrificed to the gods in order to have a good performance. Perhaps they danced around a goat onstage. Perhaps singing tragic songs sound like the braying of goats. We don't know! What do you think?

EXERCISE EL3:

Research the following plays or movies and decide if each is a tragedy or comedy, and circle your choice.

Then, create your own list of at least three tragedies and three comedies.

1. *Moana*   Tragedy/Comedy

2. *Westside Story*   Tragedy/Comedy

3. *Oedipus Rex*   Tragedy/Comedy

4. *Willy Wonka and the Chocolate Factory*   Tragedy/Comedy

5. *The Crucible*   Tragedy/Comedy

6. *Star Wars*   Tragedy/Comedy

7. *Shrek*   Tragedy/Comedy

8. *Twelfth Night*   Tragedy/Comedy

9. *Les Miserables*   Tragedy/Comedy

10. *The Importance of Being Earnest*   Tragedy/Comedy

TRAGEDIES	COMEDIES

REVIEW

Write a Latin sentence in the following format. Your sentence may turn out to be very silly, but it should function as a sentence together. Then translate your sentence.

_________________________ !
INTERJECTION

____
PRONOUN

____
VERB

____
ADVERB

____
NOUN

____
CONJUNCTION

____
ADJECTIVE

____
NOUN

_________________________ .
VERB

_________________________ ?
INTERROGATIVE

Translation:

\-

\-

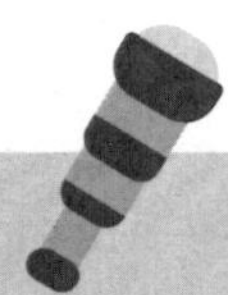

ZOOM IN

Graffiti has been around since ancient Rome, but even now some of it is written in Latin! In 2017, protesters spray-painted Latin graffiti on the side of new houses in England. The message, "Locus in domos, loci populum!" meant to say, "Local homes for local people"—though the grammar was incorrect. It was a protest against people moving to the area. Why would opponents of the new homes choose to make their point in Latin?

GLOSSARY

a/ab—prep. away from

ad—prep. to, towards

ago, agere—v. to do, drive

ambulo, ambulare—v. to walk

amo, amare—v. to love

aperte—adv. clearly

arbor, arboris—noun, f. tree

arma, armorum—noun, n. (pl). weapons, armor

aqua, aquae—noun, f. water

aut—conj. or

avia, aviae—noun, f. grandmother

avus, avi— noun, m. grandfather

bibo, bibere—v. to drink

bellus, bella, bellum—adj. pretty, handsome

benigne—adv. kindly

bene—adv. well

bulla, bullae—noun, f. amulet

breviter—adv. for a short time

calceus, calcei—noun, m. shoe

capio, capere—v. to take, to seize

caput, capitis—n. head

care—adv. dearly

caseus, casei—noun, m. cheese

caro, carnis—noun, f. meat

celeriter—adv. quickly

centum—num. one hundred

circum—prep. around

cur—adv. why

dea, deae—noun, f. goddess

decem—num. ten

deus, dei—noun, m. god

dico, dicere—v. to say, talk

discipulus, discipuli—noun, m. student

diu—adv. for a long time

domus, domus—noun, f. home

duo, duae, duo—num. two

e/ex—prep. out of

ecce—inter. look

edo, edere—v. to eat

educatio, educationis—noun, f. education

ego—pro. I

eheu—inter. oh dear, alas

eo, ire—v. to go

et—conj. and

eugepae—inter. hooray

exercitus, exercitus—noun, m. army

facile—adv. easily

facio, facere—v. to do, make

famelicus, famelica, famelicum—adj. hungry

familia, familiae—noun, f. household

fatigatus, fatigata, fatigatum—adj. tired

felix, felicis (gen.)—adj. happy, blessed

fenestra, fenestrae—noun, f. window

ferociter—adv. aggressively

festum, festi—n. festival

fibula, fibulae—noun, f. buckle, pin, brooch

filia, filiae—noun, f. daughter

filius, filii—noun, m. son

floreo, florere—v. to flourish

fortunatus, fortunata, fortunatum—adj. blessed, lucky

frater, fratris—noun, m. brother

frigidus, frigida, frigidum—adj. cold

frumentum, frumenti—noun, n. grain, crops

fugio, fugere—v. to flee

gladiator, gladiatoris—noun, m. gladiator

gladius, gladii—noun, m. sword

gratia, gratiae—noun, f. thanks

habeo, habere—v. to have

ianua, ianuae—noun, f. door

ille, illa, illud—pro. that/those (he, she, it)

imperator, imperatoris—noun, m. emperor, general

in—prep. in, at

insula, insulae—noun, f. apartment

inter—prep. between

invenio, invenire—v. to invent

iratus, irata, iratum—adj. angry

ita—adv. so, thus

iterum—adv. again

laetus, laeta, laetum—adj. happy

legio, legionis—noun, f. legions

lente—adv. slowly

lupus, lupi—noun, m. wolf

magister, magistri—noun, m. male teacher

magistra, magistrae—noun, f. female teacher

magnus, magna, magnum—adj. big, great

male—adv. badly

mater, matris—noun, f. mother

me—pro. me

mihi—pro. to me, for me

mille—num. one thousand

mirabilis, mirabile—adj. wonderul, marvelous

minime—adv. not at all

miles, militis—noun, m/f. soldier

miser, misera, miserum—adj. sad, miserable, wretched

mortuus, mortua, mortuum—adj. dead

nihil—noun. nothing

nomen, nominis—noun. name

nos—pro. we

novem—num. nine

novus, nova, novum—adj. new

numquam—adv. never

nunc—adv. now

octo—num. eight

omnis, omnis, omne—adj. every, (pl.) all

optime—adv. great

palla, pallae—noun, f. shawl

panis, panis—noun, m. bread

parvus, parva, parvum—adj. small

pastor, pastoris—noun, m. shepherd

pater, patris—noun, m. father

patrius, patria, patrium—adj. paternal

pax, pacis—noun, f. peace

pessime—adv. horrible

per—prep. through

pilum, pili—noun, n. javelin

piscis, piscis—noun, m. fish

placidus, placida, placidum—adj. peaceful

populus, populi—noun, m. people

potestas, potestatis—noun, f. power, ability

puella, puellae—noun, f. girl

puer, pueris—noun, m. boy

pugno, pugnare—v. to fight

publicus, publica, publicum—adj. public, belonging to the people

quaero, quaere—v. to look for, search

quamquam—conj. although

quando—cong. when

quantus, quanta, quantum—adj. how much

quattuor—num. four

-que—conj. and

quinque—num. five

quis, quid—inter. who, what

quod—conj. because

quot—adj. how many, how much

res, rei—noun, f. thing, affair; state

respondeo, respondere—v. reply, answer

rex, regis—noun, m. king

regina, reginae—noun, f. queen

salveo, salvere—v. to be well, healthy

scutum, scuti—noun, n. shield

sed—conj. but

semper—adv. always

senator, senatoris—noun, m. senator

septem—num. seven

serenus, serena, serenum—adj. tranquil

sex—num. six

sitiens, sitiens—adj. thirsty

solea, soleae—noun, f. sandal

solus, sola, solum—adj. alone

sonorus, sonora, sonorum—adj. loud

soror, sororis—noun, f. sister

specto, spectare—v. to watch

spectator, spectatoris—noun, m. spectator

statua, statuae—noun, f. statue, image

stilus, stili—noun, m. pen, pencil

stola, stolae—noun, f. dress

suaviter—adv. sweetly, pleasantly

sum, esse—v. to be

sub—prep. below

super—prep. above, over

tabula, tabulae—noun, f. writing tablet

tacitus, tacita, tacitum—adj. silent

tandem—adv. finally

te—pro. you (singular)

templum, templi—noun, n. temple

tu—pro. you (singular)

tibi—pro. your, to you, for you

timeo, timere—v. to fear, to be afraid

toga, togae—noun, f. toga

tunica, tunicae—noun, f. tunic

trans—prep. across

tres, tria—num. three

triclinium, triclinii—noun, n. dining room

tristis, tristis, triste—adj. sad

ubi—adv. where, when

unus, una, unum—num. one

valeo, valere—v. to be well, healthy

validus, valida, validum—adj. strong

valide—adv. powerfully

venio, venire—v. to come

verus, vera, verum—adj. true

via, viae—noun, f. road

video, videre—v. to see

villa, villae—noun, f. country house, villa

virilis, virile—adj. manly, mature

vinco, vincere—v. to conquer

vinum, vini—noun, n. wine

vos—pro. you (plural)

veterani, veteranorum (pl.)—noun, m. retired soldiers

virilis, virile—adj. manly, mature

vinco, vincere—v. to conquer

vinum, vini—noun, n. wine

voco, vocare—v. to call

volo, volare—v. to fly

vos—pro. you (plural)